CHRISTMAS

BEYOND

MONTPELIER

CHRISTMAS BEYOND MONTPELIER

F. ROSS PETERSON

Probitas Press
Los Angeles

Published in the United States by
Probitas Press, LLC, Los Angeles
www.probitaspress.com
800.616.8081

Publisher's Cataloging-in-Publication Data
Names: Peterson, F. Ross, 1941- .
Title: Christmas beyond Montpelier / F. Ross Peterson.
        Description: Los Angeles, CA : Probitas Press, 2024. | Includes 89
        b&w photos. | Summary: Ten true stories from the author's
        life, exploring what Christmas really means in terms of family life,
        travel, education, and civil rights.
Identifiers: ISBN 9798988281269 (hardback) | ISBN 9798988281276 (pbk.)
Subjects: LCSH: Peterson, F. Ross, 1941 – Biography. | Christmas. |
        Families. | Adoption. | Education. | Civil rights. | Utah –
        Description and travel. | New Zealand – Description and travel.
        | BISAC: BIOGRAPHY & AUTOBIOGRAPHY / Memoirs. |
        BIOGRAPHY & AUTOBIOGRAPHY / General. | TRAVEL / General.
Classification: LCC CT275.P48 A3 2024 | DDC 920.71 P—dc23

Christmas Beyond Montpelier recalls ten true stories from the author's life.
Continuing with the Christmas spirit, Ross explores what Christmas really
means in his life.

ISBN 979-8-9882812-7-6 (softbound)
ISBN 979-8-9882812-6-9 (hardback)

Cover photo: Utah State University in winter
Book Design by Mickey Fryer
Photos courtesy of Ross and Kay Peterson

ProbitasPress.com | Fax 323-953-9850 | Office/text 800-616-8081
2016 Cummings | Los Angeles, CA 90027
ymaddox@probitaspress.com

10 9 8 7 6 5 4 3 2
Printed in the United State of America

CONTENTS

INTRODUCTION

During the COVID pandemic (2020), I was encouraged to publish a series of short stories about Christmas in our hometown, Montpelier, Idaho. Originally written for our children and grandchildren, many friends urged us to publish them. Thankfully, Lee and Yvonne Roderick convinced us and then prepared them for publication.

The response to the book, *Christmas in Montpelier*, amazed, surprised, and inspired us. In writing about the period between 1945 and 1960, I ignited a flood of memories from many readers who recalled similar circumstances. Although told through my imperfect eyes and behavior, each story found advocates. Our Montpelier friends have been both receptive and appreciative. Many former students and colleagues who had never heard of Montpelier, found joy, humor, and even some sadness in the stories.

We have returned to the Bear Lake Valley numerous times to speak at class reunions, book groups, and civic clubs. While extolling the significance of personal stories as an important way to examine historical events, we remind audiences and readers that each of us has and is a story.

To fulfill our annual commitment to our family of a new story each Christmas, I wrote many that do not pertain to Montpelier. For the most part, Kay and I have lived most of our sixty plus years of marriage near Logan, Utah, and Utah State University. That is where our marriage began and where we continue to live, even in the winters.

However, a variety of opportunities allowed us to live in many other areas. The set of stories presented in this volume focuses on those unique experiences, as well as others in Logan. Kay and I have been blessed wherever we lived by so many friends of all descriptions. When we married in 1963, I could not have imagined the breadth and depth of the life we continue to share.

This volume begins in Logan and follows us to Graduate School at Washington State University in Pullman, Washington; our first employment at the University of Texas in Arlington, Texas; and our return to Utah State University in 1971.

Many of the stories focus on later Christmases away from Utah, such as a Fulbright Fellowship to New Zealand, a sabbatical in Salt Lake City, and then three years as President of Deep Springs College in California. One story is based on a pre-Christmas weekend in Albuquerque, New Mexico, with total strangers. Our lives are enriched by how Christmas became a treasured memory at each stop of life's journey.

Finding a Christmas story in each locale is easy, but much different from the simple stories of my youth. Mischief, chores, and routine changes with age and responsibility. Adult life is more complex and hurried.

However, it is still a time to have fun and seek pleasure in being with kindred spirits from throughout the world.

In re-reading the stories, I am reminded of how the foundational experiences of being a child in Montpelier, shaped our lives, beliefs, and actions as adults. Christmas remains the core that holds these stories together.

A quotation from Franklin Delano Roosevelt continues to guide us. "We must scrupulously guard the civil rights and civil liberties of all citizens, whatever their background. We must remember that any oppression, any injustice, any hatred, is a wedge designed to attack our civilization."

Obviously, Christmas is not the time when all of life's events occur. The message of love, inclusion, and understanding the impact of Jesus' teachings means the spirit of the holiday can be part of our daily lives.

When we are faced with professional, religious, family, and friend's traumas, we find ways to navigate with kindness and honesty. These stories refer to the passing of our parents, siblings, Bart's wife, Jen, and our recurring confrontations with cancer of many varieties. Some of these events intersect with the Christmas season, but all are a reminder that we remain connected in a woven fabric network of family and friends.

There are three life changing experiences that are missing from these pages. I tried for years to somehow relate them directly to Christmas and failed.

The first is the eight years I spent as a Bishop in the LDS church. My best friends to this day are the youngsters that taught me so much during the 1970's in River Heights, Utah. I allude to it in the story called "Christmas Connections", but I cannot believe the complexity of that calling. The church and the people, and especially my family survived it, but so much of what you do is personal and confidential.

Leonard Arrington, the LDS church historian and a mentor asked me to keep a diary because they did not have any modern bishop's journals in the church archives. Two weeks into the calling, I phoned him and said, "No thanks." Twenty-five years later I served again in a married student ward on campus. I atoned for earlier mistakes and developed life lasting commitments to a new set of friends. They too, continually document that education matters. This excites me and make me proud.

Secondly, Utah State University's Alumni Association asked me to lead historic tours which Kay and I have done for nearly thirty years. They are never in the winter, but we return each time with a renewed gratitude for our nation, its citizens, and its past. These friends and our shared involvement enabled us to navigate many of life's temporary roadblocks. Those tours gave us the knowledge of how to organize and then deliver a fantastic journey with family and friends in the summer of 2007. That is the basis for another story: "A Christmas Like No Other: 'Take Me Out To the Ballgame.'"

Finally, the many students that have enriched our lives deserve stories and I hope to write them. When I chose to teach as a profession, I did not realize that an assessment of my success is the lives of students. They continue to make me proud through their commitment to continually enhance their part of the world. This includes my three sons, whom I taught, as well as my grandchildren. They know that the Christmas message transcends all boundaries. We learned those principles as children in a small town called Montpelier.

Since I started writing the stories, three of my siblings have passed. Donna Lee (2008), Max (2018), and Karl (2021). I miss them constantly. (There are many reasons, but fact checking is an art that is needed, and they were the best.)

The main reason we returned to northern Utah in 1971 was to be near family. Texas was good to us and the decision to leave proved difficult. But the reality of close family proximity was a most precious luxury. It was very important for us to be near home during my parent's quick and unexpected deaths and Kay's dad's as well. Kay also took great care of her mother, aunts, and their friends. Living close to my sister and four brothers for decades was a bonus. Jennifer (Bart's wife) became gravely ill with cancer (2020). Since Bart's family lives in California, distance and the inability to help as much as we wanted, haunted us.

However, my youngest brother Brent, lives within an hour of Bart and he was there for every trip we made. When Jen passed in 2022 our entire family shared a major loss. Now, Reed, has moved to Logan, so my former partner in mischief is close by and a joy in every way. Brent also has a home in the valley, so an enclave of Atlanta Braves fans knows when, where, and how to congregate. With the help of grandchildren, we are quite good at streaming athletic events.

Please enjoy these stories of Christmas through the adventures of one family. Then, take a deep breath, fine tune your memory, and find time to write your story.

However, I suggest you be careful if you publish your experiences. Utah State University's Theatre Department is producing *Christmas in Montpelier* as a solo theatre show this Christmas (2024), starring my friend and colleague, Richie Call. That is a scary proposition.

F. Ross Peterson

Logan, Utah 2024

Buggy Date

THE GIFTS OF LIFE AND DEATH (1963-64)

Written 2019

In 1888, the Utah Territorial Legislature chose Cache County as the site for a Land Grant College. Cache County borders Idaho and is over 400 miles from Utah's southern border. The local citizens recommended the bench east of Logan, near the city's cemetery, overlooking the recently completed Logan Temple. It is not clear if anyone of those founding settlers had ever walked from the crest of the hill east toward Logan Canyon on a November morning. Those fall canyon winds have been a chilling reminder for over a century to every student who attended Utah State University. When I have asked alumni "What about USU do you miss the least?" The answer is almost unanimous: "Those bitter morning canyon winds in the fall and winter!"

To this day, I love those winds. They trigger memories of student days, avoidance strategies, classroom selection decisions, and how to humble faculty members. During the Winter and Spring quarters of 1963, I lived with two friends from Montpelier, Ralph Busco and

Del Lyons, in a basement apartment on Second West and Fifth North. Before I bought a car, I walked straight up 5th North to Old Main and avoided much of the wind. Later, I parked on 7th East and climbed the 126 stairs to the building, then fourteen more up the front porch and into an inviting warm hall that led to classrooms.

I returned home from a mission for the Church of Jesus Christ of Latter-day Saints to the Midwest determined to be a professor, but I had no clue of what to profess. Two history classes, one from Stanford Cazier, the other from Brigham Madsen, sent me directly on a path to teach American History. Once an academic course seemed exciting and attainable, I started to enjoy college life, especially Aggie basketball. One of my friends from southern Idaho, Phil Johnson was a senior on the team and with Wayne Estes and Troy Collier, they had a NCAA tournament team. Weirdly, although still 5'10" I decided to start playing again.

I spent two weeks scouting all the student LDS stake basketball games and picked the USU Second Ward which met in the Institute and needed an unselfish point guard. Boyd Christensen from Grace, Idaho and Hank Rawlings from Preston had both come back from missions, so Hank's brother Dick recruited us. We won the local tournaments and spent a week playing in the All-Church Tournament in Salt Lake during the quarter break. Once spring arrived, I expanded multi-tasking to include dating.

One day in late March, I ran into JoAnn Bauman from Montpelier on campus and asked what her high school friends were doing. She mentioned that Mary Kay Grimes was a sophomore at BYU and we laughed about reclaiming souls from the "parochial school south of Orem." Kay and I had been friends since grade school and whether it was playing softball, instruments in the band, writing for the student newspaper, or just having fun, we shared a giant comfort zone.

Before I called her, there were two problems that had to be addressed: the first was about her commitment to BYU and the other was her deep affinity for the Brooklyn, now Los Angeles, Dodgers. As a Milwaukee Brave fan, the Dodgers were a nemesis with only one redeeming feature, Jackie Robinson, and the integration of baseball. Once I found Kay at a Heritage Hall dorm phone, she quickly deflated my strategy by telling me she was leaving for model UN meetings in San Francisco and would be back in a week. Her abrupt dismissal of my attempt to see her, spurred my interest.

Once she got back to Provo and I went to visit, every other facet of her amazing being overshadowed her questionable educational and baseball "fanatic" choices. It is honestly difficult to describe a courtship that started as children and never wavered. We spent about four weekends with a variety of friends in various places and the sparks became flames. Shortly after the end of school, both of us returned to Montpelier for the summer. We decided that the Christmas season was a good time to start a partnership with eternal ramifications. I had a great summer road construction position running a concrete batch plant for Jack B. Parson Construction and Kay worked at the local IGA store. The plans unfolded and a tiny savings account slowly grew.

During the summer, we agreed that my becoming a professor was more urgent than Kay's taking over the U.N. so we agreed on attending USU. The Dodger-Brave problem evolved into a less significant issue for her. Her passion for the game and the players who excelled overrode a devotion to one franchise. Besides, she had Sandy Koufax on her squad, and I had Henry Aaron. That alone can be a foundation for a great marriage.

In September, I went back to Logan, and she continued to work. In retrospect, it might have been best to get married in the fall. However, Christmas is a festive time and it sounded great. My brother Max and Karen got married in December, so there was precedent. Kay's high school friend, JoAnn Bauman and her intended, Lynn Davis, also decided on December. We chose the sixth and they the thirteenth.

Since my lone assignment was to show up, I never knew if Kay lost a coin toss, a dice roll, card cut, or granted them the next week because their hometowns were Geneva and Samaria, both in Idaho. Since the towns are separated by over 100 miles. JoAnn deserved two receptions. The Christmas season got crowded, so I prepared to do as instructed.

Two weeks before the wedding, Kay suffered a back injury and came to Logan to see a specialist. Her cousin, Dee Ann Brown, and her family lived in the island area of Logan and Kay stayed with her. Her appointment was early on Friday, November 22, so after my eleven o'clock class, I raced to a pay phone on the first floor of Old Main and called to see how the appointment went. She came to the phone and almost reverently, reported, "Someone shot President Kennedy!" As I listened, I realized that she was reporting what she was seeing on live television. Parkland Hospital, Dallas, the Stemmons Freeway, were etched in the crevices of my brain.

Stunned, I hung up and walked down the basement to my German class. When Prof. Valentine Suprunowicz, a Russian immigrant married to a Polish Math teacher, came in she quietly dismissed the class by saying, "Our President is dead. He meant so much to those of us who love peace." I sat with my study partner, Grant Vest, and we visited for the hour.

I reminded Grant of something that only history students should know: every president since 1840 elected twenty years later (1860, 1880, 1900, 1920, 1940, and now, 1960) had died in office.

The remainder of the fall quarter is a blur. For some reason, USU and Utah played the scheduled football game the next day in Logan. Most colleges canceled their games and although snowy and very cold, USU and Utah chose to play. Snow was piled into the area behind the end zone and along the sidelines. I took my two younger brothers, Reed and Brent, to the game as the wind howled out of the canyon. The Aggies lost 25-23, ended a 8-2 season, and no one seemed to care.

We drove to Montpelier through a fierce canyon storm. Everything seemed gloomy, sad, and even, bad. The next day, Sunday, I called Kay to check on her at home and she announced, "Some guy just shot Oswald." She was watching live television again as Jack Ruby shot the suspected assassin, Lee Harvey Oswald, while surrounded by police. Suddenly, Thanksgiving, Christmas lights, and even weddings fell under the dark cloud that covered the world. The funeral procession, riderless horse, the young family, Arlington National Cemetery, and the eternal flame became the compelling national focus. With the rest of the nation, we could not stop watching.

December 6 was a Friday, and the fog in Logan was as dense as I have ever seen. At 6 a.m., I picked up Kay at the Brown's house and we inched up the hill to the Temple. We worried about whether any of our family could get there, but by the time the ceremony started, our families were with us. Pictures on a freezing foggy day were out of the question and I wished the canyon winds could clear out the valley. The only way we found the sun was by driving up the canyon for our wedding breakfast, at the Zanavoo Lodge, which started at about 3 p.m.

Sometime in the middle of the festivities, I remembered that my final paper in German History was due at 5 p.m. When I appeared at Professor Doug Alder's house at 4:59, he just stared in disbelief while Kay laughed in the car. She stopped laughing when I drove to the USU Trailer Court and showed her the pad where our first home would sit and informed her that we could not get anyone to move the trailer until almost New Years.

We had a reception in Montpelier the next evening. (The weather is the reason a wedding in September is preferable!) During the next two weeks, I went back and took my finals, we went to the other receptions, and finally opened and then exchanged multiple duplicate gifts. Consequently, our first Christmas was only different in that I now could stay over at her house after everyone else went to bed.

Moving the trailer from Montpelier to Logan was a nightmare. The truck came from Salt Lake City, hooked the old trailer on and began a winter trek through Logan Canyon. When we arrived at pad #10, it was covered by well over a foot of snow, so with borrowed shovels, we cleaned it off and the driver backed the trailer into place. He did it with precision and accuracy. I handed him a check for the agreed amount, and he announced, "You're supposed to pay in cash." He followed us to a bank on Main Street and I raced in at about 4:59 again, under considerable stress; and paid him $159.00.

Finally, we took a deep breath, walked down Main Street surrounded by the Christmas lights and decorations and were happy. The next day, we arranged with Karren Oil to come and connect the oil barrel on a stand near the trailer to the furnace. Then I crawled under the trailer and carefully screwed the water source to the copper tubing leading into the trailer. I asked Kay to turn the water taps on at the sink and let me know when water appeared. The valve turned easily, but I kept it at low volume and waited for her shout signaling success. Suddenly she screamed. "Turn it off!!"

Obviously, the previous owners had not drained the copper tubing and water had frozen. The floor quickly flooded. The outside and inside temperature was very cold and despair filled our hearts. As we surveyed the scene, there was a quick rap on the door. We opened it and a Christmas angel walked in and said, "Hi. I am Theo Thomson, your neighbor, welcome to the world of trailers. What can I do to help.?"

A trained electrician, Theo had talent in areas I had never dreamed of, and he explained that he had re-plumbed a number of trailers and we could start on ours tomorrow. We sadly returned to the island and asked Browns if we could stay. For the next two days, he worked nonstop and as his 'gopher," I watched and fetched while he put all new tubing in and then rewired much of the trailer as well. Four days after we moved the trailer onto the pad we finally moved in, emptied the trunk and back seat of the car, and asked Kay's folks to deliver another load. Our savings and checking accounts still had enough to pay for Winter Quarter, but we had a roof and a home with sides that rattled with the slightest canyon wind.

Kay and I thoroughly enjoyed our eighteen months in the trailer court among a hundred other families, all pursuing a dream and living in a reality. There were ups and downs, but we adjusted and learned that student body cards provided an amazing window to all that occurs at a university. We both secured student employment in Old Main, Kay in the Art Department, and I as a Teaching Assistant in Stan Cazier's USU History survey. Kay's position in the Arts and Humanities college gave us access to plays, musicals, concerts, and art exhibitions. Our desire to be on or near a campus was reinforced. Every day we walked to and from campus together, through the Logan Cemetery, and continued the courtship.

The time in Old Main taught us to appreciate good teachers, faculty that cared about students, and how to maneuver around academic egos. One morning, after class, Dr. Cazier said, "I need you to do me a favor." Thinking in terms of exam questions, study groups, or checking sources, I replied, "Yes, Sir. Anything." I quickly learned to never say that again. "Thanks, you will present the lecture in class on April 20!" Then I remembered it was April 1 and I waited for "April Fools." It did not come. He said they were expecting a baby and his wife had scheduled a C-Section delivery on April 20 in Salt Lake City. Since they had lost a child earlier, this meant a lot.

As a junior in college, twenty-two years old, I questioned nothing he said, but internally, I thought, "He has lost his mind." Cazier was a fantastic lecturer, students never missed his classes. Earlier in the quarter, he leaned against a table and in mid-sentence, the table collapsed, and he never missed a word. Most students, busily scratching notes, never even knew he went down.

When he told me the topic, for April 20, I about died. Utah had passed a state Americanization curriculum requirement that said every college had to provide a one quarter course in American History. Cazier combined two Quarters of US History into one by talking faster. My topic was the American Transportation Revolution in the first half of the nineteenth century. I could have had abolition, the westward movement, the era of reform, and he gave me steamboats, canals, rivers, roads, and railroads. My solution was to tell the students why he was gone, the passing of an earlier baby, and asked them to take a moment and silently wish him the best. One student had the audacity to ask, "Will what you say be on the exam?" I answered, "I chose the multiple-choice questions for each exam." I lectured for fifty minutes, and they did not even take notes.

Jobs in Cache Valley were tight in the summer, so we moved back to Montpelier and worked a variety of construction related tasks. We started to study PhD programs and we thought a lot about where we wanted to spend the next few years after USU. During the summer, we learned that our family would expand sometime between Christmas and early January. When we returned for our final year in Logan, the Fall of 1964, excitement was in the air.

Kay continued to work in Old Main but chose not to go to school pregnant. I still had the undergraduate TA position ($1 an hour), but also became a custodian in the Family Life Building cleaning up the pre-school nursery type rooms in the basement. I went in at 5 a.m. and worked for two hours (Minimum wage: 80 cents an hour). Wilson Elementary School hired me as the noon playground supervisor ($1 a day plus my lunch). Two of my high school friends, Marcia Meek and Patricia Sorensen were teaching at Wilson and much to their later chagrin, vouched for me. My brother, Karl, hired Max, who had returned to work on a Master's Degree, and me to referee LDS church basketball games in the Smithfield Stake (three games a week for $5 a game- toughest job in creativity.) Religion ended as soon as the teams prayed for "sportsmanship, no injuries, and to get home safely." Then they fought, yelled, screamed, and swore! Sadly, that describes the adult men.

Our old friend, the constant morning canyon winds welcomed us back as well. Kay stayed at home and helped me with all of the assignments, so I drove the car and parked it in the "Golden Toaster" church parking lot east of campus. Then I could run and jump in the car after my 11:30 class and get down to have lunch before the children gathered on the Wilson playground. I could get back for a 1:30 class unless there had been playground casualties. Speaking of injuries, Hazel Adams, the Wilson School principal, fired me twice. It was not that children got hurt, but they got hurt playing the games I taught them. Foursquare and hopscotch and jump rope seemed a bit tame, so the playground games learned and perfected on the rock pile called a playground at the Washington School in Montpelier were introduced to the fine young children on Logan's Island. Some broken arms, concussions, and one broken leg resulted, very similar to ones I witnessed and experienced in my own character-building elementary days. Whenever I see Gary Smith, Orrin Olsen, or the Calderwood brothers these days, I simply say, "Don't bring it up."

On a Sunday morning, October 18, 1964, an earthquake shook Cache Valley and the Golden Toaster church where I was blessing the sacrament in the Junior Sunday School. The Sacrament table decided to do a fox-trot dance step to the west, and I about fell on my chin. After slight aftershocks, everyone went home and examined some minor damage to things falling from the wall. The newspaper wrote about the severe quake of 1962 that did considerable damage, especially to the old Logan Junior High down on Federal Avenue. We were reminded that all of Utah's major universities are constructed on a fault line.

A few weeks later, in the early pre-dawn hours, the east winds literally went berserk. When this happened, a trailer is a disaster waiting to happen. I have always thought that tornadoes warm up on a trailer court before they take on a big, more challenging, target.

Kay hated the sounds of the wind and the rattling, cans careening down the road. Other flying debris necessitated nighttime moves to a more stable facility. We had arranged with either Max and Karen or Charles and Patricia Sorensen to come across 1200 East and stay on their couch in Aggie Village. Karen was also expecting, so one night we went to the Sorensen's. Shortly after we settled in, someone started pounding on their front door. Charles answered the door to greet our Trailer Court neighbor, Mike Whitworth, who asked in a calm and quiet voice, "Are the Petersons here?" I ran to the door and Mike slowly said, "Ross, you better come. Your trailer is about to blow over." Charles, a handyman in his own right, grabbed a bunch of things including pulling chains and ropes, and we followed Mike back to the trailers.

It was pandemonium! Garbage cans were flying, pieces of metal came right at you, people were trying to do anything, and everyone was yelling about this trailer or that one being destroyed. Some had blown over and disintegrated. We pulled my 1956 Chevy up next to our trailer's east side and began chaining the frames of the vehicle to the trailer. Since the original pads had no anchors through the concrete, most trailers had been moved away from the pads which meant some water or oil lines had broken, but there were no fires. Our trailer, chained to the car, began to weave and drag the car sideways.

The winds continued as everyone began to check on neighbors and friends. I do not recall a police officer, fire, or even university official present—only friends and neighbors checking on each other. The LDS Bishop, Charles Kleinman, opened the church and told everyone to go there with their children. One couple could not remember who they handed their baby to as they watched their trailer tip over, but the child was later located.

Once the winds subsided after about nine a.m., an assessment began. Seven trailers had been destroyed, many other damaged and destined for condemnation, and even the roof of one of the Aggie Village units had partially torn away. The steeple on the toaster church, loosened by the earthquake, toppled through the west chapel roof and severely damaged the interior. Since phone, electric, and water service had ceased, I ran to campus to inform the administration that we needed help. I also raced up to the History Department and asked the secretary to please call all my bosses and tell them, I am AWOL for good cause.

Many university personnel came by and surveyed the scene. Our trailer had little damage, but I kept it chained to the car. Very few people had insurance policies and the university admitted negligence by not following guidelines about anchoring trailers when they constructed the court. Many professors came by and offered their homes as a refuge and those who had lost their trailer became the focal point as we tried to gather as much as possible of their belongings.

Trailers do not disintegrate with style. They are made with cheap materials and the internal frames are less than sturdy. Many professors met with community leaders, and they started a relief fund and secured temporary housing on campus or in the community. Bishop Kleinman got his home ward to provide lodging as well and many stayed until Christmas with local families. These angels of mercy also made sure that every family had a place to go for Thanksgiving while they simultaneously secured clothes, bedding, and toys for Christmas gifts.

The university improved each pad by installing at least four anchors chained to the frame. The money raised by the university community paid for most of the repairs to individual trailers and provided for skirts to be installed around the bottoms to help prevent freezing pipes. Those who lost trailers accepted university housing but were not very interested in getting another trailer. Those canyon winds were not going anywhere.

As Christmas 1964 approached, we already felt genuinely blessed to still be in our little home. We decided not to travel anywhere for the holidays because either Logan or Emigration Canyon was not where a person needed to start feeling labor pains. Dr. Gasser told Kay the baby could arrive any time, so we hosted a few festivities.

Christmas day arrived and Kay's folks and siblings drove down from Montpelier. In direct opposition to 1963, it was a clear and warm day, so Kay's dad and brother, Larry, decided to bring their golf clubs and play nine holes at the Logan Country Club. There was hardly room for people. With a small tree, presents, a crib, and one tiny miniature bathroom, it was tight. Our hearts and minds totally focused on the arrival of our own baby as the celebration of Jesus' birth passed.

This baby thing was a new experience for both of us, but I could not help but think of how my dad could tell when an animal was about to give birth. One time, when Kay could not hear, I called Dad and asked him how he could tell and what should I watch for as a rookie. He laughed as only he could and finally simply said, "Animals don't wear clothes." He always knew that of his five sons, I was the worst at anything on the farm. I knew and he knew that the minute I was gone, farming was gone. Later, I spent three years at Deep Springs College wishing I had watched and learned more from him.

We timed the drive from the trailer court to the Logan Hospital on three different routes depending on the weather. It was between about three and a half to five minutes. That made me feel better. With so many young married couples in Aggie Village and the trailer court, it was a well-worn path. Since Max and Karen also expected a January baby, we often loaded their boys and us in a car and rode past the Hospital, down into Logan to see the decorations on Main Street and feel the spirit of the Christmas season. With so little snow, it was strange, but that changed with the New Year.

Kay awakened me about 5:00 a.m. on January 5 and said, "I think it is time to go see what this is all about." She was calm and had her bag packed for her stay. We had no idea of the sex of the child, but what they wore home was secondary. I could not time the sequence of her contractions, but just loaded the car and drove.

In 1965, birth in a hospital was not a real shared experience in that for much of the time, the mother is on her own with hospital personnel. The co-perpetrator of the occasion is often isolated in ignorance waiting to be told any news. On the way to the hospital, I mumbled encouragement and love, but really was clueless about how Kay felt. After she was admitted and examined and carted off to a room, Kay asked me to call her folks and tell them that we were on our way. Once again, I found myself at a pay phone, calling them collect, because I was saving my dime to call the "bosses" about my being absent again. In retrospect, I should have waited awhile because Bret (8 pounds and seven ounces) took thirteen hours to show up and be welcomed in the late afternoon. We went to the hospital in the dark and he obviously waited to be born in the dark.

I was able to spend most of the day with Kay and then wait while a false alarm played out and I waited. I did not wander very far or even go to the bathroom for fear that I might miss an update. Love and empathy filled my soul as Kay went through the delivery process and I sat or stood dazed. There is no doubt the greatest Christmas gift is the birth of a child. This shared experience gave a new perspective on Mary, Joseph, and the stable with no doctors, nurses, delivery rooms and warm lights—only friendly animals and a few angels.

The next month proved a spectacular time of love and learning. Kay was alone most of the time because of my many jobs and working around classes. At one point, it appeared that I may have to go to summer school to finish and then one of the professors suggested I transfer my transcript nonsectarian LDS Institute credits to make up the difference. Interestingly, I had never thought that was a possibility and a few years later it was not. If I was going to miss a class, it was the Institute classes, so when I checked my grades, the transfer would lower my GPA. You have to work hard to not get an A in an Institute class, but I obviously succeeded. We decided to wait until all my graduate school materials were submitted before transferring the credits. Kay spent January typing graduate school applications as I worked to pay the fees.

My greatest domestic service was to accept the responsibility to gather cloth diapers from Kay's hands and put them into the toilet bowl. I gracefully thrust the diaper into the freezing toilet bowl and then scooped, slid, scraped, or rolled the residue into the toilet. Then after a flush, I did all I could to squeeze the water from the diaper. This necessitated using both hands to squeeze before arthritis set in and then the second flush. With hands turning blue from frostbite, I opened the diaper pail for the final deposit. Then I washed my hands in the hottest water available. Kay fired me from direct changing duty because I was less than quick in covering a certain appendage while removing the tight diaper. A few shots to the face and clothes only meant more work for Kay. The fact that I pierced him a couple times with the diaper pin hastened my dismissal. I was relegated to the bowl and pail.

We loved going to the USU basketball games more than anything. The old George Nelson Fieldhouse, which was not that old in 1965, was a raucous place. Max and his family had all gone with us, but we missed the January games. I asked Kay if I could go to the game USU was playing against Denver on February 9. Kay gladly sent me on my way to watch Wayne Estes, as a senior, attempt to score his 2000th point in an Aggie uniform. His roommate, Del Lyons, was from Montpelier and a great friend, so we knew Wayne well. The Denver Pioneers had boasted that they would not allow him to score the necessary 47 points. Well, he did, plus one—48. The second his last shot hit the bottom of the net the crowd erupted and people would not stop screaming. Wayne was removed from the game as the bench mopped up a victory. On the way home, I cut through the Logan cometary to give Kay a recap. Of course, she had been listening. We visited while we sealed the last of my graduation applications and finally went to bed.

The next morning, before I left for the Family Life Building, I turned on the radio. Wayne Estes had been electrocuted the night before by a live wire. A car had crashed on 400 North and in getting out to observe the damage, he hit the wire with his forehead. Although it was a sketchy report, I woke Kay to tell her. Bret awakened during the conversation, and we held him tight.

As I drove to the parking lot, my mind went back to my feelings after Pres. Kennedy's assassination fifteen months earlier. Death is death. Accidents or assassinations cause death. At the peak of performance, during a time of triumph and excellence, still so young, lives were taken. In trying to grasp some meaning to these horrendous events, a Historian has been taught to ask, WHY? The questioning word is not applicable in these circumstances. There is not a why! I love reading the poetry found in Ecclesiastes, but I struggle believing there is a time and a season for a shortened life. A few days later, the Fieldhouse filled again as the campus and community joined in a memorial service. All-American, 2001 points, college graduate, friend.

Between the time of the two traumatic deaths, John F. Kennedy and Wayne Estes, we celebrated a wedding, the birth of a son, and unparalleled joy. We also reflected on two Christmas seasons designed to bring out the best in all humanity.

Life is lived and loved and why it ended at 46 for JFK, 22 for Wayne Estes, or 33 for Jesus, we cannot change. I do know that they, in their way, chose how to live their lives in a manner that made my life more meaningful. Most significantly, their lives and deaths, tie me to Christmas in a unique way. The foundation for a marriage, family, and career was shaped through the events surrounding their lives.

Each Christmas season we can pause, reflect, and remember the goodness we see around us. That reality helps us move forward with a renewed commitment to be likewise. The canyon winds still come in the mornings of the fall and like so much of life, remind us of what is reliable and memorable.

President Truman's Office at the Truman Library

GRAND HOLIDAY JOURNEY
Written 2020

The sun rose quickly over the rolling hills above the Fairway Student Housing in Pullman, Washington. Another October day dawned in the Palouse as I poured our two-year-old son Bret's Cheerios in response to his 6 a.m. wakeup call, "I woked up! I want my cereal! I want my cereal!"

We lived in a prefab duplex east of the campus of Washington State University, just a quick ten minute walk to my graduate office. As I approached the office, I noticed a sheet of paper taped to the door. Not knowing if the note was for me or my office mate, Tom Noer, I carefully opened it to read, "Mr. Peterson, please come to my office this morning." Signed, Dave Stratton. As the Chair of my dissertation committee, Dr. Stratton's note created an immediate anxiety in me. So rather than race across the walkway to his office in Todd Hall, I sat at my desk and tried to think about how I had maybe "screwed up."

My first thought focused on the class I was teaching, my first class-Civil War to the Present. After I passed my comprehensive exams, Stratton, Elmo Richardson and the

Department Chair, Ray Muse, called me back to Muse's office. They told me to consider a Public History, non-teaching position, because "my personality did not lend itself to teaching." Stunned, I walked away and did some serious soul-searching. When I arrived at home, I talked to Kay and we agreed on a plan. My dream (and hers) had always been to have me teach.

The very next day, I went back to my committee and the Chair and made a proposal. I offered to give up my tax-free NDEA Fellowship with its additional dependent stipend ($4000 total) for an opportunity to teach a survey class of my own ($2700). I also reminded them that I would not seek a teaching job until my dissertation was finished, since I had by-passed a Master's degree. Kay agreed. They accepted my proposal and I was given one section, Tuesday/Thursday, 3:30-5:00. Maybe the students had complained, but how could they judge me in one month? Both professors had attended one of my lectures and seemed pleased.

Still in a daze, I walked over to the office complex and found Stratton, who summoned Richardson, and I awaited my fate. Richardson could be intimidating and was known for flunking candidates at the time of their comprehensives. A brilliant lecturer, I watched him, knowing that if there was an axe, he would wield it.

David Stratton, a soft-spoken beloved mentor asked, "Are you going on the job market this year?"

Puzzled, I responded, "I'd like to but I promised to wait until I finished the dissertation."

Pausing, I was going to add something about their comments last May about a teaching career, but Richardson exclaimed, "We think you'll make it! This is a good year to get a job."

Stratton added, "You have a real head start but you need to go to the Truman Library in Independence, Missouri to polish off your research."

Since I was teaching, I answered, "I'll go as soon as winter break begins."

"That is best. We'll try to find you some travel money, so check the schedule and make your plans. We believe you can do it." Stratton concluded the meeting.

I called Kay and said, "It looks like we are not spending Christmas in Pullman." We had already developed a letter to send to prospective university History Departments which we now sent with an inserted paragraph to some within reasonable distance of Independence, Missouri.

We then embarked on the wildest pre-Christmas escapade in our history. We sent letters to our parents in Montpelier, Idaho; Mel and Shanna Talbot in Boulder, Colorado; Mike and Sheila Whitworth in Kansas City, Missouri;

and the Truman Library in Independence. After hearing that the University of Arkansas and the University of Texas at Arlington were interested in visiting with me, the plan expanded in its complexity. In the days before bank cards, cell phones and computers, we developed a ten-day pre-Christmas December agenda that involved automobiles, trains, airplanes, buses, rental cars and more of the same.

On an early Friday morning, December 15, we left Pullman before daybreak and began a one-day journey of 630 miles in our 1967 Mercury Comet (complete with snow tires). We circled around a Central Idaho snowstorm by going southwest to Pendleton, Oregon, picking up a yet-to-be-completed I-84 (then 80-N), turned east over the snow-covered Blue Mountains through eastern Oregon on to Boise.

As usual, Kay had stashed enough food and blankets to cross the plains and in pre-car seat restraint days, Bret had a warm bed and play-area in the back seat. We had picked up a Phillips 66 card, so we gassed up whenever we saw a station and still made it to Montpelier by 8 p.m. Kay insisted we turn left to drive east on Main Street in order to see the lighted blue spruce trees in the median and get the "true feel" of Christmas.

The next morning, we went to the small Montpelier Union Pacific passenger depot and I purchased an open round-trip ticket to Denver and back. Ticket in hand, I called the Talbots who had recently moved to Boulder from Kent, Washington and told them my arrival time. I have often thought how presumptuous it was that I assumed our friends would drop everything and pick me up and then deliver me. They did— bless them!

By Saturday evening, the train reached Cheyenne, Wyoming, where I changed trains. In Denver, Mel met me and drove me the thirty miles to their home in Boulder. The huge train station was decorated for Christmas and filled with holiday travelers. There was new snow on the ground as we traveled to their home. One thing I knew about Shanna Talbot—we would eat fine fare! My wildest hopes were fulfilled as she brought out a pan of stacked enchiladas followed by her signature pear pie. My favorites!

The Talbots overlapped with us only one semester at Washington State, but they became our fast friends. Shanna introduced us to Mexican food (which has become a life-long addiction!) and Mel provided space at his lab for me to study German and French. Our Colorado visit lasted well into the night and the next morning they all took me to Stapleton Airport for my first ever commercial air flight. They went right to the gate with me and I secretly wished I could just stay with them!

The Continental Airlines flight to Kansas City was crowded and boisterous. Many passengers smoked nonstop after takeoff, and in all honesty, I think I prayed the entire two hours. Why would anyone leave their family, fly in an airplane and jeopardize their future, especially at Christmas, for a few footnotes, quotations, and job interviews? Insanity! Airplanes used to circle a long time before landing and after a seemingly endless approach, I was in an intense attitude of sitting prayer, too shy to kneel.

Mike Whitworth met me at the gate. His ever-present smile and soft voice welcomed me. Our neighbors in the Utah State University trailer court during our undergraduate years in Logan, Mike and Sheila were now in Kansas for Mike's second year of medical school. Sheila was Kay's Uncle Harry's sister and we had known each other since childhood. In addition, the Whitworth's were both from southeastern Idaho, which made us soul-mates.

When we got to their festively decorated Kansas City apartment, Sheila and their young son, Jeff, joined us to see the Christmas lights of downtown Kansas City. Christmas was in the air, in spite of no snow.

"Mike, I think three days is all I need at the Library. I have to be in Fayetteville, Arkansas by 8:00 Friday morning and then Arlington, Texas by 1: 30 that afternoon."

Sheila questioned, "You mean you don't have tickets?"

"There really was nowhere to buy them in Pullman, Washington and I thought I could figure it out while I am here."

Mike interjected, "Sheila's great at this. Let her work on it!"

Our plan from Monday through Wednesday was simple. Move Mike, in his car, to the medical school in the morning and then just keep going east on Independence Avenue until I came to the Truman Library. It opened at 8 a.m. and I stayed until it closed at 5:00. Then I drove back to Mike's school and waited until he was ready to come home. We usually bought some food on the way and then he studied into the night.

I left Sheila some money and she had some ideas on how to get me to Arkansas and Texas. The hitch was that I might have to spend a night in Joplin, Missouri on Highway 71 in order to catch a bus that arrived in Fayetteville by 8:00 a.m. We looked at the map and followed the road south from Kansas City to Fayetteville. As my finger crossed Anderson, Missouri, I remembered the Cunninghams, Kay's Dad's cousins, lived in that southwest corner of Missouri near the Oklahoma and Arkansas border.

"Does the bus stop in Anderson?" I asked Sheila.

"We can call tomorrow, but that looks tiny." Sheila answered.

Mike looked up from one of those forty-pound medical textbooks and chuckled. "This is as crazy as when our trailers almost blew over. You hardly know those folks." (Our trailers in the USU trailer park did almost blow over in the fall of 1964 when tornado-strength winds blew in and wreaked havoc with the student trailers. We both had very vivid recollections of that shared episode!)

"When the Cunninghams were last in Idaho visiting, Jack said, 'Y'all come see us, ya hear!' I'm about to take them up on their offer!"

For three days I went through every file in the Truman Presidential Library that pertained to the former Idaho Senator, Glen Taylor, the 1948 Presidential election, and how Truman handled those who opposed his effort to contain Communism. There was also an intriguing section on Truman and Taylor's efforts to advance Civil Rights. The files on McCarthyism proved valuable and by staying at task, I finished by Wednesday afternoon. Every day I walked by President Truman's office to see if he was in, but the days were cold and icy and his gatekeepers said he was staying at his home.

In the meantime, I called the Cunningham's and they seemed excited that someone from Uncle Charlie's Idaho clan would come to see them. They had been in Idaho that summer and we had met them then, so it was not a "cold call." Simultaneously, Sheila bought a bus ticket to Anderson that left Kansas City at 6:00 a.m. and arrived at 9:30 a.m. She also bought a ticket from Anderson for the next morning that reached Fayetteville at 7:40. If I had not been as concerned about saving money, I just should have taken the Thursday bus all the way to Fayetteville.

As it turned out, the slight delay in Anderson was definitely worth it.

The last night in Independence, we went to a shopping area and I bought some Chiefs and A's memorabilia. Unfortunately, the A's 1967 season was their last in Kansas City, so (fortunately for me!) the prices on their hats and shirts were at rock bottom. The Chiefs were the hot AFL team that year, and that helped with the Christmas spirit.

The Whitworth's were glad to load me on the bus early the next morning, but before I left, they decided to take the train home for Christmas and we arranged to meet in Denver on Saturday night for the final leg back to Idaho. I left some of my purchases with them so I could travel lighter, thinking only of myself.

Jack Cunningham met me as the bus slowed to an "almost" stop in Anderson on Thursday. He had taken a day off work and decided to show me the area along the Missouri-Arkansas border. Although tired, I had a delightful day.

The highlight was a trip to the National Military Civil War Battlefield at Pea Ridge, Arkansas, an amazingly pristine beautiful field where armies fought in March of 1862. Three

Confederate Generals were killed as the Union forces secured Missouri for the Union. On a cold December morning, Jack loved telling me the story as we toured the field alone. Becky invited Grandpa Charlie's sisters and a few cousins to dinner and we had a Missouri Christmas feast.

Very early the next morning, Jack waved down the bus and I, clad in a suit, tie, long raincoat and polished shoes, climbed aboard. The bus was on a "milk run" which meant it made five stops, including Bentonville and Rogers, before unloading me at the Fayetteville bus depot about 6:30 a.m. Two women were behind the counter in the tiny lobby which was filled with cigarette smoke and the aroma of coffee. There were no signs of the Holiday season.

"Young feller, are you lost?"

"No, ma'am. I need to go to the university."

One of the ladies took a long drag and said, "You should of got out back a mile or two."

I had only a small suitcase and a briefcase, so I replied, "Can I walk there by 8:00?"

"Hell yes, unless you're a damn turtle." Then they laughed.

I had checked my cash and decided I could afford a cab. "Is there a cab service to campus?"

"At this hour! Boy, you better start walking." More laughter. "Why are you here?"

"I am interviewing for a job at the University."

"Well, son, stick your nose in the air and get a dress hat because you don't look like one of those "high falutin" phonies!"

Just then a cab pulled up. The driver jumped out and yelled, "Who ordered a ride?" The two ladies laughed and pointed at me.

The same cigarette/coffee combination encompassed me in the cab. The grizzled, but pleasant, young driver loved the Razorbacks, and offered to wait for me until after the interview to take me to the airport to catch my flight to Fort Smith and then to Dallas. The Christmas lights of Fayetteville reminded me of the season, even without snow.

History Departments are usually in the oldest building on campus and Arkansas was no exception. Their location was in Old Main, like Utah State. I met for an hour with the Chair and two other professors. We went through my resume and interests as well as a few other things about my dissertation. Although they were courteous, I left knowing that I was not on their radar. Though I had been invited to come, they had been clear that 8:00-9:00 a.m. was the only time they were available.

The cab driver whipped me to the airport. I quickly jumped into a small, maybe twelve passenger prop plane that made the sixty-mile flight to Fort Smith where, at the flight attendant's instructions, I walked across the tarmac to a slightly larger plane that had its engine running. I do not recall a boarding pass, seat assignment, nor certainly not anyone going through my luggage. The small planes did a lot of jumping around in the air which I assumed must be normal, but again, prompted lengthy prayers that included a few sincere promises and an occasional attempt at repentance.

Landing at Love Field in Dallas was an emotional event. It had been only four years since President Kennedy's assassination, and he too, had landed at Love Field on that fateful day. I noted the airport's many Christmas decorations as I grabbed my suitcase right at the plane and found the rental car area. This was my first attempt at renting a car, so I went to Hertz, showed them my driver's license, pulled out some cash ($8.95), signed the documents and walked out of the terminal. Crossing the street, I found a new two-door Chevrolet.

Time was short as I followed my map through Dallas. I went south on Westmoreland until I connected with Interstate 20, which became a toll road. Cash was becoming an issue, but I had enough change to get off on the Cooper Street Exit and drove south to the University of Texas at Arlington campus, which straddled Cooper. I parked at Texas Hall, crossed the street and asked the first person I saw, "Where is the History Department?" It was 1:25 and my appointment was at 1:30. The individual replied, "I have no idea."

The Library was in front of me so I charged into an old building on my left and saw "History and Philosophy." It dawned on me, I had not eaten all day. I probably looked like death warmed over, had bad breath and smelled like smoke, which a quick glance in a restroom mirror unfortunately confirmed.

"Hello, I am Ross Peterson, and I have an appointment with Dr. Barksdale."

"Yes, I am Glynnie LaPlante and Dr. Barksdale said for you to visit with the Dean, Charles Green, and he would meet you there. The Dean's office is in the Library, Room 134." She was the most pleasant and helpful individual I met on my trip. The weather was very sunny. I had not even looked to see if anything resembled Christmas. Actually, I started to sweat as I entered 134.

"Good afternoon, may I help you?" Introducing myself to the secretary, I was ushered into the most tidy office I had ever seen (a speck of dust would have no one to talk to). The Dean was dressed "to-the-nines" for a Friday afternoon at a university in December! His handshake did not resemble a grip and he immediately began talking about why faculty should live in Dallas.

Arlington had only been a university a short time and this was the first year in the UT system and Austin hated branch campuses. Dallas had opera, theatre, Neiman Marcus Department stores and wonderful restaurants. He never mentioned the Cowboys! This went on for about twenty minutes and suddenly he stopped, "Oh, Dr. Barksdale is here. Thank you for coming." I stood up to shake his hand, but he had already turned and opened a file cabinet.

Barksdale greeted me, took out a wooden match, and struck it on the base of Green's lamp. With a hand-rolled cigarette dangling from the corner of his mouth, he lit the smoke, took a deep drag and muttered, "Don't believe a word that lying S.O.B. told you! Let's go." Green did not look up and Barksdale did not look back. Neither exchanged Holiday pleasantries.

We walked across the small quad to Barksdale's office where he extolled the greatness of Arlington's future—the town, the university, the new airport, and the people. He grilled me about my dissertation and Glen Taylor. When I paused for a breath, he said, "We need survey teachers. Texas law requires every student to have two semesters of U.S. History and one of Texas History. Can you teach?"

"Yes, sir!"

"Are you going to come whining about not being able to teach your specialty?"

"No sir!"

"Lyndon Johnson is and always will be a mean S.O.B. I hate that cruel man! Why in the h--l are we in Vietnam? Is that why you wrote about Taylor?"

"Well, he would not have liked this War."

"We are going to hire at least five U.S. Historians. Will you move to Texas?"

"Yes, sir."

"I want to beat the market, so you will know by January 15."

He rolled another cigarette, rubbed his scruffy chin, squinted at me and concluded the interview. "We need gut-busting, a-- kicking liberals in Texas. This university is growing and I refuse to teach in any room over 70, so students can't get history courses, I send them screaming to the Dean and I get five new teachers!" He cackled more than laughed and told me to fill out some forms with Mrs. LaPlante, "just in case."

On my return to the airport, I decided to retrace President Kennedy's motorcade route, see the Texas Book Depository and drive north on Mockingbird Lane to return the car. When I stopped the car by the curb and looked up at the window where Lee Harvey Oswald shot the rifle, emotional exhaustion set in. Dallas had trees and street poles all decorated with lights. The reality of Christmas descended on me and I cried.

The car returned, I walked into the terminal, making my way to the Continental counter to check in. The flight was to Oklahoma City, with a continuation to Denver. The large jet's route avoided turbulence and so with rental car and commercial air experiences under my belt, I prayed a bit less fervently on the return flight.

The Talbots met me at Stapleton and took me back to Boulder. I had left them on Sunday and now it was late Friday night. Colorado had a lot of snow and we talked about that we were glad that driving across Wyoming was not in our plan. (We did drive it the next year, but that's another story altogether!) I relayed my few days' adventures to them and finally ate something, with a pear pie dessert.

The next day Mel took me back to the train station where I met the Whitworth's for the journey to Idaho. The engineer on the Union Pacific streamliner navigated the Medicine Bow mountains as we slept. Mike and Sheila had been on the train all night. Each Wyoming town had Christmas lights burning as the train completed its 500-mile journey.

Staring out the train window, I recalled that five years earlier I had made this same journey returning from a mission. The rhythm of a train is good for contemplation and visions of home. This Christmas season gave me an opportunity to see friends and relatives, enjoy their generosity and bask in the love of the season. While traveling down the tracks, I wrote thank you cards and felt a deep sense of satisfaction in completing an insane journey through, above and around ten states.

In those short few days, I got the material I needed to finish the dissertation, interviewed for two positions and accepted an Assistant Professorship position at UT-Arlington. More importantly, the time of year refreshed a commitment to friends and family. Following a fantastic family holiday in Idaho, we looked for a break in the weather to take the automobile ride back to Pullman. What a grand Christmas journey!

The new Michael McLean song, "12-25-365," (which he added to his "Forgotten Carols" in 2017) is a reminder that Christmas is always a part of us. Exactly 50 years following my grand journey, I appreciate this beautiful reminder.

*Mike and Sheila Whitworth moved to Tulsa, Oklahoma following medical school. He had an illustrious career as a surgeon, They traveled with us on some USU Alumni tours. Mike passed a few years ago.

*Mel and Shanna Talbot remained in Boulder, Colorado. A brilliant chemist, Mel spent his career in Colorado. Shanna surely made her award-winning pear pies until their deaths.

*Jack and Becky Cunningham have now sadly passed away. But we did see them at the home of Aunt Dorothy and Uncle Harry in Star Valley, Wyoming where we had many laughs about Ross' grand adventure.

*Glynnie LaPlante proved to be the conduit for the adoption of our much-loved son.

*E. C. Barksdale taught me to never stop fighting for students. I tried to avoid embracing his colorful vocabulary. I was only somewhat successful. . .

*The two Ladies from the Bus Depot in Fayetteville, went to work at Waffle House.

Ross Graduation, June 1965
Kay, Bret, Ross

Abe Grimes, Gean Grimes,
Kay, Ross, Zora Peterson,
Raymond Peterson.

Cutting the cake.

Ross with Professor Stan Cazier.

E.C. Barksdale, University Texas Arlington, Department Chair

David Stratton, History Professor, Dissertation Director

Bret on tricycle, East Fairway, Pullman, WA

Mike (holding Andra) and Sheila Whitworth.
Jeff Standing on right.

Mel & Shanna Talbot
Boulder, Colorado

Front row: Otto Puempel, Curtis Mclean, Bob Brey, Brad
Kelly, Lan Jones.
Back row: Gordon Duncombe, David Von Boss, Mark
Emmick, Ross.

BASKETBALL, RELIGION, and the "LATTER-DAY REBELS"
Written 2009

My fingers tentatively caressed the keypad of my cell phone. This was not really a cold call, but after forty years, it caused great nervousness. Slowly, I hit the area code, then the next seven digits—the phone rang once (it seemed like an eternity); twice, a long pause; a third time, and I waited for the voice mail to take over.

"Hello," the voice was deep and melodic. "Curtis McLean?"

"Yes. To whom am I speaking?"

"Curtis, this is Ross Peterson, in Logan, Utah. How are you?"

"Dr. Peterson," then a pause, "are those mountains still high?" I imagined the huge smile on his face.

We exchanged inquiries for nearly half an hour and promised each other that we would stay in touch. It is a long way from Logan, Utah to Bowie, Maryland, but there is no excuse for not staying in contact, especially when we had been so close for one school year forty years ago. When Curtis said, "Dr. Peterson," in that still familiar voice, my memory focused on the moment I first heard it.

September 1969 Arlington, Texas, my second year of teaching at the University of Texas Arlington. The beginning of a new class is always somewhat stressful and on this muggy, hot day it seemed uninviting as I imagined the commuter students only looked at a required U.S. History course as one more hurdle. I knew I had to provide the passion.

After reviewing the syllabus, emphasizing the writing required, apologizing for textbook costs, and giving an almost unbelievably profound and exciting overview of the semester, I asked the obligatory inquiry, "Are there any questions?" Hearing none, I cheerfully added, "OK, I'll see you on Thursday."

"Dr. Peterson," a clear deep voice could be heard above the clamor of students preparing to leave.

"Yes, sir?" I asked.

"Are you a Mormon?" Suddenly, everyone in the room froze in their positions and a hundred pairs of eyes focused on me as I looked up at my inquisitor. He was tall, handsome, clean cut and African American.

"Yes, sir, I am," I answered.

"Why can't I have your Priesthood?"

No one moved and suddenly this first day of class was already different.

"This is not something that we should discuss in a classroom, but I will certainly do so in private," I responded.

"When?" he asked, with a voice neither threatening nor angry, just determined. He cocked his head, stared and waited. His voice was not threatening nor did he seem angry.

Amazingly, no one had left the room.

"Come up to my desk and we will set a time to get together." Now the rest of the class left except for a few other African American students who had taken the first half of the required two-semester U.S. History course from me the previous summer. They seemed somewhat shocked and followed the inquisitive student to the lectern.

"What is your name?" I inquired.

"Curtis McLean—I am a sophomore Music major from Fayetteville, North Carolina. When can we meet?"

Before I could answer, both Audrey Prince and Willie Salisbury began to defend me as a teacher and advisor. We had worked together on a concerted student effort to change the school nickname from "Rebels," as well as to have upholstered sofas with offensive slave scenes removed from the Student Center.

Curtis calmly reiterated that while he appreciated the positive reviews of my teaching skills, he still could not understand why he could not have the Mormon Priesthood and wanted an answer.

We set a time to meet in the evening with the condition that I would drive him to Fort Worth where he lived with his brother's family. I invited the other students to come as well, but they declined, while again defending my works over my faith's theology.

Thus began an amazing personal relationship. The problem for me was that by 1969, I no longer even believed the discriminatory policy, let alone defended it. A year earlier, after the assassinations of Dr. Martin Luther King, Jr. and Robert Kennedy, and the debacle at the Democratic National Convention, my wife Kay and I discussed our theological dilemma with Senator Frank Church of Idaho. (Following a campaign swing to our hometown of Montpelier, Idaho, Senator Church was having a late evening haircut in Abe Grimes'—Kay's Dad's—barber shop.) After listening to my lament about the LDS Church's position on the Priesthood, he observed simply, "You cannot change something by leaving it." Senator Church continued with a brief lecture on the necessity of effecting change from within. We totally embraced that idea.

That is where I started with Curtis. He was an exceptional scholar of the New Testament, so from the beginning, it was Jesus against the prophets: Old Testament, Book of Mormon, and modern day. As we visited, I learned that his knowledge of Mormonism was based on random information from a colleague who sang with him during the summer at Six Flags Over Texas, an Arlington amusement park. Mark Emmick, a recent convert to Mormonism, knew enough to be really dangerous; especially when he delved into scriptural curses that affected skin color or theories of pre-existent behavior determining earthly birth status. At best, these ideas were tough to defend, so I did not.

After an hour of discussion, I became eager to change the course of our conversation. As a counselor in the Bishopric of the small Arlington Ward, I offered an invitation to Curtis to sing in an upcoming church service. His answer, "No, sir, how could I do that?"

"Look, we need to educate people and let them accept each other. If they do not know you, how can their ideas change?"

"What is this, some kind of mission?" he laughed.

In the fall of 1969 a tense racial atmosphere prevailed in both the community of Arlington and in the LDS church. When the Wyoming football team's black players boycotted the annual Wyoming vs. BYU game, it became national news. UT Arlington's black students had removed the offending furniture from the Student Center and there had been a massive march and peaceful demonstration against "Rebels" at a football game. The primary target was the huge "Stars and Bars" which comprised the entire back of each marching band uniform.

The university administration blamed me for encouraging the students to toss the sofas into the courtyard. That was only partially true—I did not advise "tossing," only getting rid of the offending sofas. Curtis was in the midst of these activities even though he worked, took twenty semester hours, and attended a weekly seminar on discrimination.

Curtis agreed to sing in the Arlington Ward in late November. I cleared it with Bishop Otto Puempel, physician, graduate of Marquette University, and a convert to Mormonism. He and his wife, Wanda, were also children of the 1960's—liberal and inquisitive, questioning always and not above challenging. And they possessed the biggest hearts in the state of Texas!

Wanda, as church organist, practiced with Curtis, giving him the opportunity to meet another family and a different home besides ours. The other counselor in the Bishopric, Jack Downey, an engineer, and a convert from New York, was also willing to "hear the man sing."

On the agreed Sunday, Curtis was to sing in our service with Mark Emmick, he had an earlier engagement with a Christmas choir in his Fort Worth church. Kay then drove to get him before our evening meeting. The two arrived at the meeting a little late and Curtis did not actually enter the chapel until he and Mark were announced to sing. He walked to the front in his stunning shimmery-silver suit with black shirt and silver tie. He maybe had a little extra heel on his shoes because he seemed to stand even taller than his 6'3" height.

As they began to sing "The Battle Hymn of the Republic," I could immediately see which members of the shocked congregation had undergone tonsillectomies. What a powerful and beautiful presentation. I must admit that I became a little fearful that Curtis might switch the words in the chorus back to "John Brown's body lies a moldering in the grave, but his soul keeps marching on!"

Although members of the Stake Presidency chastised Otto for "having a musical number that was not in the hymn book," Otto maintained that "it was in the hymnal." After the service, many people sought out the young singers for congratulations. Then Gordon Duncombe, a Canadian who had recently moved to Texas, stood directly in front of Curtis, measuring him up and down. There was total silence.

Finally, Gordon spoke, his eyes riveted on Curtis, "Do you play basketball?"

Otto and I sighed in relief. Jack Downey burst out in laughter. Mormon basketball is not known for a capacity to increase spirituality, let alone enhance brotherly love.

"What are you doing to me?" Curtis asked. "I do not have time for all of this."

"Curtis, this would be good for our congregation," I offered, "and we can have fun, win games, and maybe go to Salt Lake City for the All-Church Basketball Tournament."

"I *would* like to see the West," he ventured.

"Well, there *is* the issue that we can play only one non-member at a time and you have to go to church twice a month."

"This is crazy. You let little twelve-year-old guys pass the sacrament and all I can do is play ball, sing, and show up!" He agreed to play.

Our Arlington team was very good, and since there were not enough wards to play weekly, we joined the Arlington City Church League. The next Wednesday night, the Mormons showed up to play with a new recruit, 6'3" Curtis McLean, left-handed, with great leaping ability and the first black man to play in the League. We had no clue that it was an all-white League, but they were all-white churches, so how naive were we?

In the month before Christmas, we won all of our games and "the Mormons and their Nigger" epithets led to fights the first two games. Gordon's fuse was very short, but 6'2" Don Williams, a PhD Accounting professor originally from Oklahoma, had a shorter fuse.

Otto, the coach and Bishop, tried to restrain his charges, while also endeavoring to convince the other ministers to not pull out of the League. Curtis just played hard and blocked a lot of shots, which led to fast breaks for the quick little white guys. New move-in Bob Bray, a 6'3" computer whiz from Spanish Fork, UT, added another dynamic to the team and we ended up winning the Arlington City League and the LDS tournament (in Texas) in March of 1970.

Every week when Curtis and I met, we also included some of the families of the ward, ate dinner, and really did not talk much about the Mormon Priesthood policy. As Christmas approached and finals at the University were over, Curtis asked for some "serious time." I feared he was going to write us off, go home and move on.

Finances were very tight for him. I was trying to help get him some federal dollars under the new Pell Grants, but school was tough. As well, his brother had three children, in addition to Curtis and his piano, in a modest two-bedroom house. Needless to say, there was stress. Curtis, one of nine siblings, missed home—especially at Christmas.

Otto and Wanda purchased Curtis' round-trip ticket home for Christmas. The night before he was to leave, the Puempels hosted their extraordinary annual Christmas party at their home. Curtis' brother and family came with him. The abundance of children in attendance prepared to re-enact the nativity, which at the Puempels, was a major production—Joseph, Mary, baby Jesus, shepherds, innkeeper, sheep, donkey, wise men, angels and songs.

Our three-month-old son, Bart, was chosen to be the baby Jesus and five-year-old Bret in his dashing bathrobe was a convincing shepherd. There was no scarcity of angels in spite of threats about behavior. All of the participants were restless and uncomfortable in hot robes, halos and various other appropriate garbs.

Then Otto asked Curtis to read the story from Luke, with a little Matthew thrown in so the Wise Men could bring gifts. When Curtis began to read, an aura of reverence filled the large family room as well as in the staging area for the actors. I was in awe as I had never really heard the story read with such power and conviction. It may have been that soul was an added ingredient, but each child moved through his/her part with reverence. And, how beautifully they sang. When we finished with a rousing rendition of "Hark the Herald Angels Sing," a spirit of joy swept the room.

The next evening on our drive to the airport at Love Field in Dallas, we started our serious talk. Curtis had been very moved by the previous evening, but he expressed a genuine reluctance to return to Texas following the Holidays. And I was in a pensive mood as every time I went to Love Field I thought of the assassination of JFK, the swearing-in of Lyndon Johnson, and the pain I felt, even years later. But tonight, the discussion was about Christmas and the baby who became the man that changed the world.

"Dr. Peterson, sir," then a long pause....

"Yes, Curtis."

"I'm just not sure that you understand what I believe. All fall we've discussed your beliefs and whether or not I fit or can fit. I don't."

"What do you mean?"

"It is Christmas. For me, it is all about Jesus. I love that all of you have been so kind, so nice, and so generous. You've tried to show me that your actions speak louder than your prophets." The teacher was becoming the pupil.

"Jesus was born, probably poor, with some degree of confusion in the hearts of his parents. Everything about the story of Christmas is about what He did and taught. His parents knew He was special, but Jesus knew that everyone, all of us, are special."

"Everything He did was for the sick, the hungry, the mistreated, the unwanted. Just think of how often He put down those who thought they were better."

I knew where Curtis was going with his narrative, and although I was somewhat uncomfortable, it was good. To listen to another's beliefs and hear their conviction is good.

He continued, "It is Christmas and we talk about His birth. The birth did not create the message. The message is in the mission. When I accept Jesus as my savior, then I must deliver the message and help fulfill the mission."

"Curtis, I agree with you, but there has to be some structure and order."

"That is where we differ. Authority and Priesthood mean nothing if they keep the message of Jesus from millions of people."

For many years, my brother Max had always talked about substance and form in religion. We agreed that when form got in the way of substance, any religion had problems. I thought of this now.

As we approached the airport, Curtis bore witness of his belief in the Sermon on the Mount, the Golden Rule, the reality of Gethsemane and the miracle at the tomb. There was no disagreement from me. Christmas lights lined the entrance as we slowly drove into Love Field.

"So, Curtis, why have you stuck with us all fall? I hope it was not just because I was your teacher."

"At first it was, a little."

Curtis gazed out the window as we approached the drop-off curb. He turned and with tears in his eyes, said, "Dr. Peterson, some day I will meet Jesus and He will say, 'Curtis, did you love your brothers and sisters?' I will look Him in the eye and answer, 'Yes, Lord, I did.'"

Curtis took a deep breath and added, "Then Jesus will say, 'Curtis, give me one example,' and I can answer, 'Lord, I spent a school year with a bunch of white Mormons in Texas whose doctrine discriminated, but whose lives spoke otherwise. I love them as my brothers and sisters.'"

Then his eyes twinkled as he added, "Dr. Peterson, I love them too, but those folks are too worried about being number one!"

We broke out in laughter. "Merry Christmas, Curtis. Please give our love to your family and I will be here to pick you up, OK?"

"Right. And, please give the Puempels my love and thanks."

The tall, thin black man disappeared into the terminal without looking back. This Christmas was complete.

*Endnote:

Curtis McLean returned to Texas to finish the school year. As mentioned, the Arlington Ward basketball team won championships of the basketball leagues and drove to Salt Lake City for the Mormon All-Church tournament. Because "Home" and "Away" uniforms were required for participation in the tournament, coach Otto Puempel tried to persuade Arlington High School to lend us theirs. Finding this impossible, we, ironically, settled for the old, no-longer used UTA "Rebels" uniforms. Because lettering was not an overnight business in 1970, Curtis played with "Rebels" stitched across his chest. He had integrated both the Arlington League and the Mormon All-Church Tournament with a true bunch of Latter-day Rebels!

Kay, Bret, and Ross at Love
Field, Dallas

Curtis McLean

Otto & Wanda Puempel

Curtis, Stella, Robin Leslie
Washington DC 1971

Frank Brocke, First Bank of Troy

Do you Believe in Angels?
Written 2022

My mother, Zora Poulsen Peterson, was amazingly close-mouthed about anything having to do with intimate relationships. She once said, "Whoever coined the phrase 'birds and bees' knew nothing about either." The week after I returned to Montpelier, Idaho from a two-plus year LDS church mission, she asked me to teach her pre-Christmas Sunday School class.

The scheduled topic in the manual dwelt on the heavenly manifestations from the angel Gabriel to Elizabeth and Mary. This can really be heavy material in the sense of divine instruction on very personnel matters. These cousins lived a few miles apart and had a wide age difference.

Elizabeth and her husband, Zacharias, were advanced in years and childless. Mary was betrothed to the carpenter, Joseph, and was probably still a teen. My mother did not want to touch this topic with a ten-foot pole, even if the mothers of John the Baptist and Jesus of Nazareth were involved with an angel.

Gabriel had a tough assignment that involved glossing over the "how" and dwelling on the "why." Perhaps he made a mistake by appearing to Zacharias first instead of Elizabeth, because when Zacharias questioned the "how," Gabriel zapped him silent until the child was born. Gabriel changed his tactic and went directly to Mary, but when she questioned him on the "how," he offered an explanation and kindly reminded her that her child was the Son of God. That took care of the "why" and he may have added "Trust me" to the rest of his instructions.

As advised, Mary went to visit Elizabeth and they discussed their calling and probable predicament. They may have even worried about what people might think. When Mary returned to Nazareth, a few months pregnant, Joseph got worried about what might be said about her and thought of ways to protect his young wife. That is when someone within the administrative unit of angels said, "Whoops, we forgot to let Joseph in on the plan!" Quickly, they utilized virtual technology and sent an unnamed angel in a dream to explain Mary's honor and Joseph's role. A good, decent, and apparently non questioning man, Joseph totally bought in on their future.

Of course, a choir of angels appeared to shepherds, telling them of the birth and two years later the new star appears in the heavens guided the three wise men to find the newborn baby. (I have always questioned the wisdom of the wise men because they went to Herod and told him what they were about.)

The nativity pageant ends here, so we never hear too much about Joseph's angel coming back in dream, instructing the young family to go west into Egypt because wicked King Herod had ordered all baby boys under two years to be slain. There is a good reason to not include this in the pageant, but the wise men were warned by an angel to not go back to tell Herod the whereabouts of baby Jesus and his family. It was a busy time for angels. The tragedy is that Joseph could not take the other little Jewish boys and their families with him. Herod's soldiers did their King's bidding and terror reigned supreme.

Just as I neared the conclusion of the lesson, one of the youngsters in the class asked: "Do you believe in Angels?" I had been telling stories about angels and answered, "Yes! They are Heavenly Father's messengers." Another young skeptic asked, "Have you seen an angel or dreamed of an angel?" The class ending bell saved me.

Through the years I have joked about the "Three Nephites", heard stories of angelic visits in testimony meetings and have seen the angel Moroni elevated to countless temple spires. Jacob wrestled with one, and other Old Testament prophets had encounters. There is no way I covet a manifestation like Saul or Alma and the Sons of Mosiah. My mother may have prayed for a light dose of angelic retribution because she felt I "made light of sacred things." Angelic dreams never came my way and honestly, there are times I need direct intervention. Promptings have been good, and a life of observation and preparation has helped. However, I have met many angels in the flesh. My angels look like normal folk who do good and inspire others to do likewise. They work year around and often shift into fifth gear during the Christmas holidays.

One of my favorite angels took care of us for ten or so years. In all honesty, he helped thousands of people through the years. Usually, bankers are not viewed as angelic because of the pound of flesh extracted as interest. Angels need to make a living, so it is not a problem to me. Frank Otto Brocke, President of the First Bank of Troy, Idaho became our divine benefactor.

When Kay and I moved to Pullman, Washington and Washington State University in the fall of 1965, the History Department chair, Dr. Raymond Muse, took me into his office and gave me a check for our Fall semester expenses, including tuition, books, fees and expenses. I had a national Defense Education Act Fellowship designed to prepare university professors. I asked Kay's brother, Larry, a law student at the University of Idaho eight miles east of Pullman, where students banked.

"Everyone I know banks in Troy."

"Troy?"

"It is about ten miles east of Moscow."

Kay and I jumped in our green 1956 Chevrolet "one-fifty" and drove east to the tiny town of Troy, Idaho, (population less than 600) and found on Main street, The First Bank of Troy.

The First (and only) bank of Troy was in a small one-story brick building with a large addition on the back. We walked through the door and saw two teller windows, one closed. We got in line and awaited our turn. The teller was an elderly gentleman, bespectacled, wearing a suit and tie. He dressed like most tellers in western movies prior to being robbed. We handed our check to him and asked to open a checking and savings account.

"Welcome to school," he said and stuck his hand under the grill to shake ours. "I am Frank Brocke."

"We are the Petersons, Mary Kay and Frank Ross." I never use Frank but chose to when he used his first name. After we filled out the forms, he handed us a book of blank checks and told us there would be some with our names and address in the mail shortly.

For the next three years, at the beginning of each semester, we repeated the process, and each time Frank Brocke stood behind the window and chatted. When I called the bank to inform them, we had changed apartments, he answered the phone. It was Frank Brocke's bank. On that first visit, we looked through an open door into the back of the building and saw as many as thirty women working on sorting and processing checks.

Frank Brocke became President of the bank during the great depression and decided to develop a relationship with the students from the two neighboring universities, Idaho and Washington State. After World War II when the area was flooded by veterans using the G. I. Bill, he took care of many young families. If possible, many banked by mail after finishing school and moving out of the area.

The bank had been robbed once. A "down on his luck logger" from Elk River, took Brocke hostage in his home and at gunpoint took him to the bank. Mr. Brocke unlocked the door, opened the till, and emptied the contents in the thief's sack. For all I know, he may have asked his abductor if he needed more. When the thief was captured and sentenced to time in prison, he corresponded his regrets to Brocke. Once released, the man came back to the area and later obtained a loan from the First Bank of Troy to start a business. One of Brocke's long-distance clients, a journalist in Los Angeles, wrote the story in the *Los Angeles Times*.

By the summer of 1968, we had finished the work for a PhD and accepted a position at the University of Texas in Arlington, Texas. We drove out to Troy to close the accounts, withdraw any funds, and move on to a new chapter. This may have been our seventh trip to Troy, but Frank Brocke talked us out of closing the accounts. "You never know when you may need us, and our checks are good most anywhere." Then he pointed into the back where his employees were busily sorting checks. "Those fine people are not playing cards." He chuckled. Frank Brocke was a wise banker and a fine angel.

The next May, 1969, I was turning in the final grades at the end of my first year at UT Arlington. It had been a good year and we just received notice that we had received a six percent raise. My base salary jumped from $9100 to $9650.

We had moved closer to campus and hoped to grow our family. Our son, Bret had turned four and it was time to learn sharing. Otto and Wanda Puempel, he was the LDS Ward Bishop, had two children older and two younger than Bret and they treated him like family. However, two sets of doctors had basically agreed that for a variety of reasons, Bret was destined to be an only child.

As I was leaving the History Department office, the secretary, Gwendolyn La Plante, said that her greatest blessing was her adopted children. I stopped and asked her, "How did you do that?" A few minutes later, I left with considerable knowledge and a phone number of a lawyer, Fred W. Davis, who specialized in Placement.

Within a week, we were in his office being interviewed as prospective parents. He worked directly with obstetricians whose patients had decided on adoption. We left knowing two things: (1) our chances were good and (2) adopting was considerably more expensive. The package included the cost of the doctor, patient, baby, hospital, and lawyer.

When I went back to the History office, I asked Mrs. LaPlante if our university insurance covered adoptions.

"Heavens no! That would be revolutionary. We asked and the company said 'we are not going there.'" It was a thought.

I had already signed up for summer school teaching, but we began to count and save and cut back on trips to Six Flags Over Texas. A few days into the next week, the attorney called requesting we come to his office. He said "We have two nice fits, one due in July and another in September. Healthy mothers and no issues."

After analysis and a realistic view of economic preparedness, we chose September. We were also informed that all parties should be paid upon delivery. The attorney told us that for the sake of privacy, the total sum of all expenses should be paid to the attorney at the time of the birth.

By mid-August, we took a full day and surveyed where we were financially. With less than a month before the due date, I prayed for an angel. I called Frank Brocke. We had not only kept a savings account in Idaho, but still wrote checks on the First Bank of Troy. Shortly after moving to Texas, we went to Minyard's grocery store on South Cooper. We approached the Customer Service window, showed the woman the check from Troy, and a card that documented I was a UTA employee and asked if we could cash a check before buying groceries. The clerk laughed out loud, and my heart sank.

"Heck yes. Anytime. I am from Deary and know Mr. Brocke." Deary, Idaho is ten miles east of Troy. Could someone from Deary be an angel?

So I called Mr. Brocke in late August.

"First Bank of Troy, Frank Brocke speaking."

"Mr. Brocke, this is Frank Ross Peterson, down in Texas." I told him the story of the woman from Deary and he knew her family. Then he asked, "How can I help today?"

I explained our situation, went through the numbers and estimates and asked if we could obtain a loan. His response is unforgettable.

"Now Frank Ross, this is what you should do. When your baby is born, write a check to the attorney for everything, including the final court fee and his fee. Keep saving, but as soon as the check is written, call me and tell me the amount. We will cover it. Then we can work out the terms and sign some documents." When I suggested we do the loan based on the lawyer's estimates, he cautioned. "There are always a few little twists, so just do as I instructed."

Suddenly Zacharias's questioning an angel came to mind.

"Sorry I asked sir. Thank you for everything. This means the world to us."

"Good luck, give my best to Mary Kay and call me as soon as you tell your families."

He chuckled whenever he used both our names. A private matter.

Three weeks later, we received a call from the attorney and informed us that the birth mother had entered the hospital. The next morning, he called and informed us that our son was ready to come home tomorrow, and we could bring some blue clothes to his office.

The next day, we pulled our car into a small parking lot adjacent to a Grand Prairie Hospital. Shortly our attorney walked through the door with a healthy, nearly nine-pound baby boy wrapped in a blue blanket. He handed the bundle to Kay and I gave him a check, written on the First Bank of Troy, Idaho. The angels had spoken. Our lives eternally benefited from this transaction based on trust.

There were at least two additional instances where Frank Brocke helped us through a temporary crisis. Neither are as memorable as the adoption of Bart, but since we had paid the note before Christmas, it made future asking quite simple.

In late March, 1971 on a Saturday morning, I received a call on my office phone. I was in the process of editing my dissertation into a book manuscript. I had been asked by Leonard Arrington, one of my USU professors, to submit to a contest. Two of my teachers at Utah State, Leonard Arrington and George Ellsworth, asked me about life in Texas and then Arrington asked, "Do you want to come back to Utah State?"

In the days before AA/OEO and job searches, that is how most universities operated. Prof. Ellsworth informed me that Stanford Cazier had been named the President of Chico State University in California and he had asked Blythe Ahlstrom to go with him as his aide. "We want you to join us."

This all sounded strange because I had just chaired a committee at UTA that recommended faculty be engaged in all national searches. Ellsworth assured me that, "We hired three new people last year, none with USU or Utah ties and just secured a Europeanist from Cal-Berkeley."

Arrington added, "We have so much happening in Western History, we need you. Besides President Taggart encouraged us to find you because you can teach African-American History."

George Ellsworth quickly jumped in to remind me that rarely does the University President recommend a departmental hire.

Since I was not talking to the Department Head and felt uneasy about the new faculty members having no say, I said, "We'll have to think about it, but I need to discuss it with the department head and at least meet the new faculty."

They pressed me a little, but I asked them to have William Lye, the Department Head, call and if anyone from the department was coming to New Orleans in April for national meetings, I would arrange to go meet them.

Kay and I really liked Arlington and had been accepted at all levels. On the other hand, an opportunity to return to a place we loved, only an hour and a half from our parents, and be near three of my siblings who lived in Northern Utah was enticing.

No angels appeared to us in person or in a dream, but after meeting Mick Nicholls in New Orleans and a having a long phone call from Pres. Taggart about what he envisioned for our alma mater, I was convinced to say yes. Then the department asked me to teach summer school as an economic incentive.

A month later, I flew to Salt Lake City to find a rental house or maybe a home to buy. Max, my brother, also worked at USU and he had scouted some areas and houses within our price range. We had an offer on our home in Arlington and felt we might have a decent down payment. Max lived in Providence and really liked a small house about the same size as our Texas home on a corner in River Heights, across from a service station. It was only five minutes from campus, less to downtown Logan, and two blocks from an elementary school. At the time, I thought it was close to Logan High School as well and it is, but River Heights is in the county, so junior high was in Hyrum and high school in Smithfield.

The real estate agent took me to a small office next to the Utah Theatre on West Center Street where a young loan officer, Kenneth Oscar Sorensen, almost insisted we buy the house and said he could find us a short term note for a down payment. He worked to get the payments down, but also reminded me he had no control over interest rates. (Later, we realized that Ken and his family lived through the block from the house.)

Although it was a Saturday, I called Frank Brocke from Ken's office. "Mr. Brocke, this is Frank Ross Peterson. Here is my dilemma."

"Wait a minute, Frank Ross. How are Mary Kay and the boys?"

"Really great sir. Thank you for asking"

Then I tried to explain quickly (I was on Ken's phone) about the move, the house, and the opportunity. My plan was to take the extra money from the sale of our house and combine with a cashed-in Texas retirement fund and pay the down payments, title fee, and closing costs.

"There is another buyer who wants the home, so there is a bit of urgency."

'Has Mary Kay seen it?"

"No sir."

"She trusts you. That is a lot of faith."

"I think she will like it, sir."

Once again, he gave me an angelic response. "Frank Ross, have them tell you exactly what it will cost to get in the house. Then write a check on our bank, mine and yours, for the down payment and accompanying costs. Once they settle on an amount, add ten percent to the total. There will always be some other expense. Call me and tell me the amount you wrote on the check and we will sign the papers when you get settled. By the way, add a little money for moving expenses."

"Thanks again, Mr. Brocke, this is a life saver."

"Not really, you just got rid of some stress. It is just a house. As long as Mary Kay likes the house, you are fine. She must really trust you." Then he chuckled again.

Within six weeks we paid off the mortgage on the Texas house, retrieved a little extra, cashed in our Texas State retirement, and depleted our savings.

"Mr. Brocke, this is Frank Ross calling. I am sending a check to cover the earlier check, but we never signed anything and I have no idea how much to send as interest."

"My that was quick. Write the check for an extra $50 and we will call it good. I don't want to figure out what a month or so of interest might be. You have a house, the bank is paid. Let's call it good."

The angel had spoken.

Even after returning to Logan, we kept an account with the First Bank of Troy. Loyalty has value and our little pittance did not guarantee success or failure for the bank. It did explain why those women in the back room stayed busy. Most importantly, there is security in a safety net.

We called upon Frank Otto Brocke a few more times, especially when our car engine was destroyed in Missouri in 1972 and I had to fly Kay and the boys to Denver from Joplin, Missouri and finish a research trip by bus until the car got fixed. That took a bit longer to pay off, but the terms were similar. "We will settle up when you get home."

In the mid 1970's we received a short form-letter from the First Bank of Troy informing all depositors and patrons that the bank had been sold, would keep the name, and hoped to continue to serve its customers. However, Mr. Brocke had been asked to step down. Apparently, there developed a fundamental disagreement over loan decisions, and an inability of trained corporate auditors to document small loans.

The fact that very few were outstanding seemed irrelevant. We finally closed our twelve-year-old account.

We wrote Frank Otto Brocke a letter and thanked him for helping us get a PhD, a son, a house, a car, and a great period of banking joy. In 1977, he passed away. At age seventy-one he took his place with Gabriel, Moroni, and a few other scriptural messengers. We still have angels in our midst and one of them is a banker.

I have not been back to the Palouse much, but one time we were at the University of Idaho watching the Lionel Hampton Jazz Festival. In between Jazz sessions I drove to Troy to see the bank. I could not resist going inside to peek at the teller window hoping to see an angel behind the bars, smiling, looking over his glasses as he cheerfully dispensed heavenly counsel on how to treat and trust each other. That he was not there did not disappoint, but memories of him filled my soul.

Yes, I believe in angels and they are my friends. At least as long as they stay out of dreams, don't strike me dumb and go easy on specific requests, the belief will grow.

Frank Brocke
First Bank of Troy

House in River Heights.

Kay holding 2 day old Bart,
Ross, and Bret.

Tarrant County Courthouse in
Fort Worth, Texas.

Fred W. Davis - Lawyer -
Arlington, Texas

Bluebird Coffee Club 12-22-00

Back row: Dick Chambers, Floyd Jarvis, Jack Laub,
Sue Davidson, Merrill Dawes, John Harder, Ben Jarvis
Front row: Jim Jarvis, Ross, Charles Bullen, Jason Hone,
Bob Rust Absent: Jim Laub, Mooch Spackman

CHRISTMAS CONNECTIONS
Written 2000

Just three more days until Christmas. Time is short and so much needs to be done. There must be a way to slow down the hours, days, and weeks of life. Time rolls by so quickly and life seems to accelerate like an out-of-control treadmill. During Friday's Christmas errands with an Open House in the afternoon and a Hanukkah party in the evening, there is an hour where time comes to a screeching halt. A few minutes at the Bluebird Café in downtown Logan. Only a brief stop-just to slow everything down. The legendary Bluebird Coffee Club is in session for an annual Christmas party with one hundred percent attendance. A few other family members and friends are invited to the Christmas function for a pleasant hour. A refuge from the turbulence of daily existence. I run to my truck and leave early for the 10 a.m. meeting.

I first heard of the Bluebird Coffee Club when Floyd Jarvis invited me down to give the members a copy of my book, A History of Cache County in 1997. The Bluebird Restaurant opened in 1914 and features a spectacular ornate soda fountain, a fancy counter, glass covered Bluebird Candy display cases, and an ancient cash register. The restaurant had no booths, just tables and chairs, and numerous dining rooms and an upstairs where most Logan Service Groups met for luncheon meetings. In the northwest corner is a room that features a three-panel Everett Thorpe mural of the historical evolution of Logan, Utah. The Bluebird Restaurant is obvious in every panel along with Logan's other landmarks, Old Main on Utah State University's campus, the LDS Temple and Tabernacle, and the Cache County courthouse.

It is fitting that five days a week at precisely 10 a.m. some of Logan's respected senior businessmen, a few professionals, and Guy Cardon, the owner of the restaurant, sit in the mural room around tables and discuss local, regional, and national problems. They playfully tease each other and never allow a topic nor an individual to monopolize the conversation. Some of the friendships extend back to grade school and they have shared the past half-century in Cache Valley. They commonly shared the Depression, World War II, and have benefited from the expanding economy of the last few decades.

For the past two years (1998-2000), I have joined them once a week and try not to be intrusive. The seating is not assigned, but the regulars have designated chairs. My dollar joins theirs in the center of the table and Jim

Jarvis, self-appointed pourer of coffee, rises and returns with a Dr. Pepper. We joke about active Mormons taking their caffeine cold. My role is to answer questions about the university, athletics, history, current events, and on a rare occasion religion. There is never a boring day.

Through the past months we have supervised the controversial 2000 presidential election and the numerous discussions of recounts, damaged ballots, and court decisions. The Club analyzed the premature departure of one university president and speculated on the selection process of another.

The group is religiously diverse, although some fear that Cal Watts is a secret member of the LDS Quorum of Seventy and that Jim and Floyd Jarvis attend different Protestant congregations in order to expand their Culligan soft water empire. Jack Laub, the Chair of the Club, is an avid reader and devotee of the history channel. After Merrill Daines and Cal Watts accompanied me on an Alumni Tour of Civil War sites, Jack quizzed them with more intensity than usually accompanies an oral exam for a master's degree.

As I turn off Logan's Boulevard onto Second North, suddenly I am hit with Christmas memories inspired by location. We were expecting our first child, and this was the route we took to time how long it took to get from the USU Trailer Court to the Logan LDS Hospital at Christmas time in 1964 (five to six minutes). The old hospital was demolished when a new one was completed twelve blocks north twenty years ago and now there is a large parking lot. It sits diagonally across the intersection northeast of the LDS Temple. The Hospital and the original Sunshine Terrace Nursing facility once occupied that now asphalt covered corner.

With memories flooding through my mind, I slowly drove the truck to the curb, leaned back and tried to visualize the events of my life that took place in those vanished structures. The buildings, owned by the LDS church, really had little architectural or historical value. However, two of my sons were born there; many friends, family, and neighbors were hospitalized; and more than a few had died there. I recalled many prayers, blessings, and tears of joy and sadness over the years, but I am always haunted by a particular memory. It involved an opportunity missed at Christmas, 1974.

It was the week before Christmas and my mother had not been feeling well. Her sixty-third birthday was on the 22nd and often got lost in the Holiday overload. She always used the Christmas season to bring joy to Montpelier, Idaho's citizens. It included extra food, music, and time for good conversation. However, she never acted alone. My Dad and all of their children shared in her efforts, so we delivered the packages, food, and even songs to the elderly, the sick, or the unemployed. Her powerful and persistent personality drew us into the pattern, often reluctantly.

I called her on her birthday to wish her well and visit. She asked, "When are you coming for Christmas?" Before I could answer, she revealed her problem and her solution. She needed someone to don the attire of Santa Claus to deliver Christmas to numerous families. According to her, everyone recognized my dad and she needed a new voice. Obviously, I had grown into the suit and she had selected me to fill the role.

"Can you come up on Christmas Eve and help us?"

I quickly replied, "I don't think we will be able to get up until Christmas Day or after, maybe not until New Years' Eve."

There was a long pause. "Why not Christmas Eve?" she asked.

In all honesty, I had a very good set of reasons and I guessed so did my four brothers.

"Well," I answered, "I've got tithing settlement, and this is my first one and we have to ask for building funds, welfare, and ward budget assessments. We have appointments and I think I need to be here." I did not mention the weather, driving conditions, children wanting to be home, or other reasons flashing through my mind. I knew I could play the church trump card and I was right.

There was an unusually long silence. She was not used to our telling her "No," and she seemed distracted and disturbed. "I guess Dad can do it, but you would be so good."

"What about Reed? He has the greatest laugh and whoever heard of a blue-eyed Santa."

She was not amused. "His boys are so young and they need him to be with them. I really wanted you."

"I'll call on Christmas and we'll visit," were my last words, and then she added, almost as an afterthought, "I have to come to Logan to see a doctor the day after Christmas, so we'll see you then."

That conversation never leaves me. Less than ten days later in that very Logan Hospital which stood on a now empty spot, she was diagnosed with colon and ovarian cancer and was scheduled for major surgery. Mother had probably not been to doctor since my youngest brother, Brent was born, twenty-five years earlier. She was old school: tough it out; fight through it; avoid expenses. I did not help to make her last Christmas one of her best.

The day before the surgery, Dad asked us to fast and pray and then give her a blessing prior to the operation. She was in horrendous pain and the prognosis was not positive. When my brothers and I joined him at her bedside, Dad surprised me by asking me to give the prayer. They had already moved her into a postoperative recovery room. We gathered there to seek divine intervention and comfort.

There is no doubt that my faith and desire and passion were for my mother to live, be treated and healed, and continue to bless us. We hoped for a positive outcome. The words of healing and calling for a long life did not come. I was not tongue-tied and thanked the Lord for giving us a "beacon of light that blessed our lives." I asked for divine guidance for the doctors and that they could be inspired to remember all that had been taught them. I asked for the strength to accept and benefit from the result through our capacity to care. That is why the old hospital haunts me, I knew the result and could not change it.

Following the surgery, Dr. Reed Broadbent came into the non-private general waiting room where we had all gathered. He informed us that her entire body cavity was filled with cancer and despite removing infected organs and doing other procedures, she was terminal. Dad was very tough, but deeply hurt. Terminal is a word that describes the inevitability of the conclusion of mortal life. It is not a kind, albeit honest, word.

For nearly two weeks after the surgery, she was in that room as she recovered and adjusted to the results of the surgery. Dad, who never enjoyed sleeping away from his own bed, drove home every day to work and do chores and then sleep and come back to the hospital. Reed, my brother just younger than I, could have easily done the chores and even cover for him at the ready-mix concrete plant he managed. On weekdays, he went over to the temple when visiting hours ended.

One day, I was alone visiting mother, and she was sitting by her window looking over at the Temple as dad slowly walked back toward the hospital. Mother had provided Dad with the only home he could remember, and he had finally conformed to her religious and personal desires. She loved him deeply and with tears cascading down her cheeks, simply said, "He is such a good man." As I left her them that afternoon, I realized that her room was adjacent to the one where her mother passed 30 months earlier.

Four months later, on Easter Sunday, 1975, she died at the home dad built for her in Montpelier. There was not going to be another Christmas so that I could atone for my insensitivity to her last request of me. Dad died of a heart attack on Father's Day, 1976. He was alone and passed in the same room and on the same bed where she had passed.

Throughout the year following her death, Dad commented many times about his overwhelming loneliness. They were 63 and 65 years respectively and deserved much more time together. I felt that my children had been robbed by their early exit. I wonder what my parents would have been like at seventy or even eighty years.

Suddenly, I returned to the present and checked my watch. The Bluebird Coffee Club beckoned, but I seemed glued to the Hospital site. I looked up to where her third-floor room had been. All I saw was blue sky. Memory drove me back to the rooms of that hospital and the 1970's. Why was I there so much and why did I drag my twelve-year-old son, Bret ,with me?

My intense relationship with hospital began earlier in 1974 when I was called to be the bishop of the River Heights First Ward. The Bishop is a "volunteer" and as part of a lay clergy, tries to understand the calling "on the fly."

The LDS Hospital's policies required the staff to call the bishop whenever a member of their congregation was admitted. They had all contact information and persisted until they found the bishop or his family. All my land lines (home, work, and church) were located within ten minutes of the hospital. Any admittance, whether an appendectomy or a severe accident, required a call. In retrospect, serving a mission, being in a bishopric in Texas, and observing office holders for years prepared a person for the call.

As I stared out at the asphalt, I recalled in one summer I had four traumatic accidents that brought me to the hospital. Rick Olsen wrecked a motorcycle up left-hand fork of the Blacksmith Fork Canyon and rode the bike into the river, near a bridge. His hand, leg, and chest were mangled, but the cold water kept him alive until a fisherman saw him and called for help. Angela Wyatt, age three, was run over by a neighbor in the intersection by our house. Another young man, Robert Kidd, got hit on his motorcycle in an intersection in Logan four blocks from the hospital. Three teenage boys, Tim Scott, Dan Farnsworth, and Allen Crockett, just weeks after being arrested for bombing fish with powerful fireworks in the Logan River, lost a hand, fingers, and an eye respectively when fireworks exploded where they worked.

In almost all cases, I got to the hospital before the parents, raced into the ER, to survey the damage. Dr. Glenn Terry, a new doctor from Tennessee and not LDS, was in the ER for all those incidents. At first, he thought I was simply bad luck and I tried explaining the role of a bishop. Sometimes, the victims asked for a blessing or a prayer, so memories are embedded deeply.

One scene reappeared that caused me to break out in laughter. One July Sabbath day, the summer after my mother died, I got a call that my five-year-old son, Bart, had been taken to the ER. He had slid down a grassy slope a few blocks from our house and a broken soda bottle filleted his bum cheek. I raced to the ER and found two nurses and Kay trying to hold Bart down while Dr. Broadbent, the surgeon who had operated on my mother, tried to stitch him together. It took 56 internal and external stitches. Worried about infection and restricted mobility, the doctor had Bart admitted to the hospital and advised a three to five day stay.

Kay stayed overnight with him, and I went up at seven the next morning. As I climbed the stairs to the second floor, I heard a commotion. I turned the corner and saw Kay and a nurse chasing Bart, attached to a stand with an IV, racing down the hall toward me. We captured the youngster as a doctor arrived to examine the squirming patient. After surveying the stitches and the damage done to equipment, he released the patient immediately.

As I finally drove away, I remembered another experience in the hospital that drained me emotionally. Shortly after our youngest son, Matthew (Fred), was born in 1977, I received a call from a young couple, Ryan and Laura Larsen, to come to the hospital. Their twin sons were born prematurely, and the doctors did not dare transport them to Primary Children's Hospital in Salt Lake City. When I arrived, Ryan asked me to assist him in giving his sons a name and a blessing. This is usually done at the church when the children are a couple of months old, so it told me the infants were fighting for their lives. As we prepared to enter the nursery, my thoughts leapt back to a similar incident six years earlier in Texas.

Otto Puempel, the bishop in Arlington, Texas, called me one day and asked me to go to a hospital in Fort Worth because a family had twins born prematurely and their chances for survival were minimal. The father met me and ushered me into a room where we were scrubbed and gloved and gowned. An official asked if we intended to baptize the babies and I tried to explain the importance of giving them a name. A nurse interrupted and said, "Whatever you are doing, move fast. There is not much time."

Once in the ICU nursery the nurses handed me the babies, one for each hand and I offered a prayer and gave them each the name chosen by their parents. Neither child weighed much over a pound. When I finished, I sat with the parents until the short lives ended. The Larsen twins were at least twice the size of the Texas babies. When I saw them, I felt a great sense of relief. Ryan and I gave them their names and blessed them to live full and complete lives.

So, the building is gone, but the memories are always there. That old facility, where thousands were born and many died, served well. Indeed, the hospital also proved to be, for me, a spiritual and educational institution. It was after ten a.m. when I at last I pulled into the alley next to the

Cinema Theatre and turned south toward the Bluebird.

Suddenly, a realization hits me like a ton of bricks. It is not a revelation, but an awareness that I go to the Bluebird Coffee Club in search of my parents. I cannot visualize them at seventy-five or eighty and beyond. This is not psychological drivel, but a clear understanding of why I love to be part of a generation that is closer in age to my parents. I cannot wait to join my friends. I am late and so I jog through a slick parking lot toward the back of the Bluebird. The Club meets before the restaurant opens, so the members enter through an inconvenient back door that is an architectural afterthought.

Today, as I make my way up the four stairs then down three stairs onto the main level. I am oblivious to the special expanded Christmas group and the conversation, reinforced coffee and tomato juice, numerous pictures, and gifts. Instead, I sit at the far end of a table and observe each of the original members and assess how to fulfill my desire to know my father and mother in their never attained old age.

To my right is Jim Jarvis, a native of Arkansas. Jim and his wife, Martha, love baseball like my dad. He, like his brother, Floyd, is a bit "unreconstructed" and was originally a railroader but came with Jim to Cache Valley and established a soft water business.

Cal Watts, whose family owned a Lumber company and a companion hardware store, is a great storyteller who rarely flirts with reality. No one could spin better folklore yarns than my Dad, so whenever Cal begins one of his sagas, I always remember Dad's tales.

Dick Chambers once owned the Fish Haven resort on Bear Lake, but returned to Logan and became a mayor. Dad served on the city council and came to dislike small-town pettiness and gossip, as does Dick.

Guy Cardon, the son of the founder of the Bluebird, typifies community loyalty and has a positive outlook on everything. He almost literally lives on campus and is a great advocate of all things art.

Wayne "Skeeter" Garrett is a quiet observant man who, like nearly all of those surrounding the tables, served in World War II. He has worked for Cache Valley Electric for years.

Charles Bullen, a former state legislator and an expert on "everything" has an irrigation company that supplies and maintains all necessary to irrigate farmland. He probably suffers the most teasing because of his positions and expertise.

When Herb Champ is in town, I am reminded of the day Dad paid of our home loan at Utah Mortgage and Loan. The drive through Logan Canyon had a special beauty that day.

Dr. Merrill Daines is the ultimate caregiver who never ceases to serve publicly and privately. My parents, children of the depression, knew suffering and sacrifice and benefited from doctor's who made house calls. Merrill still does. Merrill and Dick ski together and usually are chided for leaving the slopes by noon before they must share with dreaded snowboarders.

Finally, there is the Chairman, Jack Laub, who organizes this traditional Christmas event and controls the agenda. He is a questioner, a truth seeker, and a doubter. Jack Laub, whose parents moved to Logan from Illinois, is the epitome of a loyal community builder. His watchword is loyalty and most of these colleagues have been with him for all their lives. I watch him closely as he makes sure everyone has been served, people are thanked, and money is gathered to tip the Bluebird employees who came early to serve us.

The Bluebird Coffee Club is a small group of friends who care deeply about each other and their community. Most of their wives chose to ignore the Club because they too perform service and support the community in their own way. Besides, they are very tired of hearing the same stories.

My late arrival meant the hour ends early for me. The past is clearer and the future less daunting. My life is enriched by associations with family, friends, students, and colleagues.

And thankfully, I still have my partner. It is never easy to be an orphan, but this Christmas I am reminded by my friends of what my parents continue to mean to me. Life is very good when we seek ways to help others, just as Jesus taught. It is all very simple.

Raymond & Zora Peterson, 1972

Logan, Utah - LDS Hospital

Kay & Fred

Dad with ready mix
truck.

Bart, Ross, Kay holding Fred, and Bret.

OUR SUMMER CHRISTMAS-NEW ZEALAND

Written 2008

A wise person once described the tradition of Christmas gift-giving as "Give and forget—Receive and remember." Our Christmas in New Zealand taught us that there is great opportunity to exhibit love and appreciation without large trees, fancy lights and numerous presents; that there is something to focusing on acts of charity, not on material gifts.

On a warm summer day two weeks after Christmas 1978, our family left the small Wellington, New Zealand airport terminal, walked across the tarmac and mounted the portable stairs into the domestic Air New Zealand 737. We left behind a terminal filled with guitar-playing, singing friends, primarily Maori, who had come to bid us farewell.

After checking the several months' worth of accumulated treasures, secured in heavily taped and expertly tied boxes, we bade tearful farewells. We had been in New Zealand less than a year, but this Sunday afternoon nearly the entire community of Porirua picnicked after church, followed us to the terminal and sang until we boarded.

Our aircraft taxied to the end of the runway, which was set between Wellington Harbor and Cook Strait (dividing the north and south islands of NZ), and we looked longingly toward the terminal. Then as the plane picked up speed, we were amazed to see the roof of the single-story terminal filled with our Kiwi friends waving and swaying. We began to sob (as if any moisture was left in our bodies!). Kay and I looked at each other, held hands and hugged and cried. The boys put their heads in their hands as the plane soared into the late afternoon sky over the beautiful harbor and banked north toward Auckland. Even Matt, just celebrating his second birthday, sensed the depth of our feelings.

The incredible adventure that led the Peterson family to New Zealand was Ross' sabbatical leave from Utah State University made possible by his award of a Fulbright Lectureship at Victoria University in Wellington. Little did we know the impact that experience would have on our lives.

This Christmas had been like no other and proved to be our most memorable. For Bret (13) and Bart (9), Christmas totally removed from cold weather, snow and sleigh riding, Santa Claus and the proverbial "sleigh full of toys" seemed improbable. But in New Zealand the celebration was all about giving and not receiving and the

Peterson boys were perfectly happy to be part of it.

The hour-long flight from Wellington to Auckland gave us a few moments to recount the gifts of the natives of the Land of the Long White Cloud. What did this Christmas really mean?

For one thing-the issue of a home. About six weeks before we were scheduled to leave New Zealand, the owners of the house we had rented in Tawa, a small commuter community north of Wellington, informed the Fulbright office that they were returning from England earlier than anticipated. The Fulbright staff in turn told us the owners were going to try to secure a place to stay temporarily, but advised us to leave sooner than we had planned.

We lamented our fate at church on Sunday and contemplated some type of early departure. Auntie Wiki, a widow, came up to us after church stating emphatically, "My home is your home. I will move in with Tillie (her sister)."

By this time in our stay, we understood that one did not insult the gift-giver. We moved in the next week. Laurie Cox, Executive Director of the NZ Fulbright Office, could not believe it. Of course, he had never dealt with the Maori Mormon Mafia (my designation) and its "Grand Don," Karewa Arthur and his wife, Chris, the ultimate "fixer."

A few days later, Karewa told me, "I sold your car." We had bought the car from him when we first arrived in the country-a 1967 red Holden, the only right side steering wheel car I ever learned to drive. "I got back what you paid for it, Mate." Although very pleased, I did not dare ask, "So what do we drive for the last six weeks?" Not to worry, the next day, a small brown Datsun appeared at our house and although there was some doubt as to its legal status, it lasted the duration of our stay.

On the occasion that we traveled to the South Island for an extended tour, Karewa said to us, "I need you to deliver a car to Christchurch. When you are finished with your tour just drop it off at "Cousin so-and-so's" dealership. Then go to the Budget Rental and Billy Parata will have a car to deadhead back to the ferry." So we basically had a free auto all the time we were "Down Under."

On the southern trip as well as on those we took to explore the North Island, Karewa would always insist we stay with "Auntie So-and-so" or "Cousin So-and-so." As part of my fellowship, the Fulbright office sent me to every University in New Zealand to give talks. They could not understand why I had so few expenses.

We learned early in our sojourn how the native culture worked in an efficient and caring manner. Just after we arrived in New Zealand, the LDS Church changed mission presidents in the Wellington Mission. The headquarters, or

Mission Home, was located in Tawa not far from our house.

A few weeks after our arrival, Rudolph and Ruth Luckau came to preside over the Wellington L.D.S. mission. (He had recently retired from Utah Power and Light in Salt Lake City, was very experienced in working with Native Americans and he had instant rapport with the Maoris.)

Three weeks after their arrival, President and Sister Luckau escorted a visiting General Authority, Loren C. Dunn and his wife Sharon on a hike to the top of Mt. Victoria, a relatively small hill in Wellington which offered a spectacular view of the harbor. Following their return to the Mission Home, President Luckau fell ill and within minutes died of a massive heart attack. When the ambulance arrived with paramedics, followed by a coroner, pandemonium broke out. Of course, Sister Luckau was traumatized and wanted to leave immediately. In a strange land far away from family and friends, her world had just crumbled around her. Elder Dunn demanded the body be released so they could make proper arrangements. The medical examiner cited New Zealand law relative to the death of foreign visitors and a debate ensued over the required autopsy.

Neither side understood the power of the Maori Mormon Mafia. Beau Moeller, the local

Maori Bishop, called me at my office at Victoria University in Wellington and asked me to join him in negotiating a truce. He picked me up and we raced back to Tawa (Bishop Moeller was a crazy driver!) in time to see a heated discussion between Elder Dunn and the local police and medical examiner. The Church authorities in Salt Lake City had advised Elder Dunn to get the body and fly Sister Luckau home as quickly as possible. She would not leave without the body and the coroner demanded an autopsy and a full coroner's inquiry.

Beau Moeller, a compassionate and caring man, also exhibited a classic Maori temper. He entered the intense debate with a curt and loud, "Everybody, please be quiet!" There was a pause and then he said, "We will meet at 8:00 tomorrow morning to settle the matter."

Elder Dunn said, "I cannot wait. I have my instructions from the brethren."

The coroner and two policemen said the law dictated their actions and they would release the body when the autopsy was finished and medical examiner's report filed.

Beau Moeller responded, "You may leave now and we will be at the police station in the morning at 8:00." The three men left.

"This cannot end now," Elder Dunn replied. "We must get this settled."

Bishop Moeller's voice was firm and powerful. "After the service tonight, we will plan our next step."

"Service! What service? We must act now. There will be no service. I have to be concerned about Sister Luckau."

"Elder Dunn, we always have a service in the home of a deceased brother the night of death. That is our Maori custom."

"Bishop, he is not Maori and there will be no service in the Mission Home."

I was racking my brain for some kind of brilliant pacifying comment as Bishop Moeller rose to his full height, put his face as close as possible to the 6' 7" Elder Dunn's face and firmly, but quietly, said, "President Luckau is a member of my ward and he died in my country and we will have our traditional Maori service tonight at 6:00 p.m. in this home."

The Elders, Sister Dunn and I stared at the floor and waited for a response.

"I'll call Salt Lake."

"The Ward will be here at 6:00 p.m. and will bring enough food for everyone. Brother and Sister Marsh (the Mission Home caretakers) will have everything ready."

I finally uttered a profound contribution, "I'm sure everything will work out."

When we left the Mission Home, Bishop Moeller turned toward Porirua where Karewa and Chris lived. We knocked on their door and asked Karewa to come outside. Neither Beau nor Karewa had the capacity to whisper and they were soon joined by Karewa's brother, Ken Arthur. While they hatched their plan, they sent me to talk to Chris to make certain all was in order for the upcoming service to be held in a few hours.

What followed that evening was one of the most amazing outpourings of Christmas good will. Well over 100 people crowded into the Mission Home and music, laughter and tears filled the room. Many folks talked about how President Luckau's introductory talk in church just a week or so ago had influenced them and how impressed they were when he opened the door for his wife or accepted hugs from strangers. Traditional Maori music was performed by children and adults alike. By the end of the evening a grateful widow expressed her thanks and we all joined in song.

President Luckau's body was released the next day and Kay flew with Sister Luckau as far as Auckland where the widow was joined by returning missionaries for their long flight to Utah. I have often recalled how that group of people exhibited unparalleled charity in behalf of a near stranger. That is an amazing gift.

I am not sure Elder Loren C. Dunn ever learned how the Arthurs arranged for the body's release or what it may have cost them. However, one of their "cousins," Ben Couch, was the national Cabinet Secretary of Maori Affairs.

We learned during our months in New Zealand that opportunity for children and protection of children is a legacy of both Christ and Maoris as well. Extended families did anything to keep troubled children in the family fold. Foster care morphed into adoption and parents rested assured that their children were safe.

A few weeks before Christmas, the U.S. State Department sent me to Thailand to participate in a seminar on race relations and ethnicity. They asked me to speak at a number of Australian universities on the way to Thailand. Once the itinerary was set, Kay and Chris Arthur, with Chris's daughters, LeeAnn and Kylee, decided to go along with me as far as Sydney, Australia and then I was to proceed on the rest of the tour alone.

We left our three sons with three different families back in New Zealand. That is when Bart stayed with the Moeller family and convinced Bishop Moeller that school was not good. He did not like the cane or the strap used for discipline. Beau Moeller took Bart with him traveling around the North Island selling signs.

After our return, Bart never went back to school. He just walked to the train station with me and once I boarded the train instead of proceeding on to school he went to a small shop and one of the "Mafia" would keep him for the day. We found this out many years later when we returned to NZ for a visit. Our friends just laughed as they told us the inside joke.

Chris arranged to stay with a "cousin" in Sydney named Rangi Parker who had left New Zealand for an employment opportunity. Along with two of her friends, all entertainers, Rangi had found herself singing in the King's Cross area of Sydney, a notorious hotspot for American troops on R&R from Viet Nam. She and her family stayed in Australia after the War.

Following my lectures at the University of New South Wales we went to the University of Sydney where Kay and I stayed on campus. We visited the sites of Sydney including the stunning Opera House, beautiful harbor and convict unloading dock. Before I flew on to Thailand, Rangi insisted we come to their home to stay with them for two or three days. Her home was a haven for Kiwi refugees trying to find work in Australia-what were two more?

Rangi's husband, Vic, had two jobs, she had one, and they fed, housed and clothed about a dozen people besides their own family. The first evening we were there she said, "Now, Brother Peterson, I want you to come with me to take Christmas packages to some folks." I replied, "Of course, I'll be glad to help."

New Zealand's economy was static and very difficult for young people (even apprentices) to find work and thus Australia beckoned. We loaded the car with a number of items, mostly shipped from New Zealand and addressed to the Parkers, but with an assortment of additional names on them. We spent the night going from flat to flat in the darkest and toughest areas of Sydney. Rangi knew where the lost children of New Zealand friends and family were and what they were doing. It was not always good.

Fearless, Rangi would barge into dreary, overcrowded pads where a tobacco cloud, the odor of fresh marijuana and a variety of other smells greeted us. She hugged each one, gave gifts and then turned to me and told them, "Brother Peterson has come from America by way of New Zealand where he has seen your families. He has a message for you." The young men stared at me as if I were a caged animal in a zoo. I looked at Rangi and she nodded her head and smiled.

I began, "Greetings from your families at home. They love and miss you. Your parents trust you to do what you know is right and remember that your Savior loves you."

No one had drawn a knife or walked out and knowing the Maori respect of elders, I caught Rangi's eye and slight nod and went on. "The message I bring is that you should serve others and not put yourselves first. At this Christmas time just do something for others. Call your families, save to go home, find a way to put

Jesus in your lives. This is the time of year to start anew."

Then Rangi invited each one to come to a Christmas party at the church and come to her home on Christmas along with all of their friends. She ended by quizzing them about others she knew were in Sydney. When we returned to the car, she made notes, told me who was related to whom and drove to the next flat. She prepped me better at each place and before the evening was over, I was encouraging couples who lived together to get married and young women to throw out abusive boy friends and for all to seek haven in the church of Rangi Parker. Some walked out, others turned away, but for two evenings we took Christmas to some lonely souls.

I believe Rangi Parker and Chris Arthur knew every young Maori living in Sydney and they would report back to the families. Selfless devotion to others is what I learned as Christmas approached during those few days in Australia.

The meaning of Christmas was not simply a specific time of year to our New Zealand friends. It was the culmination of generosity of heart that they practiced year-round. The songs changed, branches of trees (not the whole tree) were decorated, multiple acts of giving of self (not presents) left a never-ending impression on each member of our family. To be sure, we gave gifts to our friends, but mostly things we had that they admired.

Kay asked one day, "How can we even attempt to thank these wonderful people? What can we do for so many? If we buy something, they will just give us something more."

As we discussed what we might do, we decided to ask Karewa and Chris what they thought would be appropriate.

They said "Do nothing." That advice did not ease our minds.

Auntie Wiki's home was small and Kay's parents were visiting with us for our final two weeks in New Zealand. Because it was summer vacation, Bret was living with his friend John Modlik in a small bachelor pad next to the Modlik home and Bart was staying in a caravan (trailer) with Scott and Owen Arthur adjacent to the Arthur's. We did not see much of the boys during these last few weeks.

The Saturday night before our return to the U.S., the Bishop called to invite us to come to his office. When we arrived at the church, we were surprised to find ourselves surrounded with the treasured friends we had made over the past months and we realized we were to be the special guests at a dinner and program.

There was so much eating and singing and speaking that everyone was filled with happiness and good feelings. We gave sincere tearful thanks and bade them all farewell. Ken Arthur then announced a special number for everyone. Tall and stately, Ken was Chief of the local Maori community and its marae (the traditional community gathering place). He had quietly tutored our sons for this special event.

"Friends, Brothers and Sisters, the Peterson family wants to thank all of us for including them in our lives. To express that thanks, I present two new Maori warriors, Bret and Bart Peterson." Two young Pakihas (Maori for white) trotted onto the cultural hall floor in full Maori regalia-grass skirts, headbands, bare-chested, each with a hand-carved Maori warrior Taiaha (spear). They then began a full fledged

MAORI HAKA

Ka mate! Ka mate!

Ka ora! Ka ora!

Ka mate! Ka mate!

Ka ora! Ka ora!

Tenei te tangata puhuruhuru

Nana itiki mai whakawhiti te ra

Upane! Upane!

Upane, Kaupane whiti te ra

Hei!

The audience went crazy, screaming approval. Two American boys, fiercely inciting the audience to do battle. They were awesome! Their chest-pounding, tongue-waggling and furrowed brows brought great enjoyment to everyone. It was our family's gift of thanks, again orchestrated by the Arthurs. Even in our attempt to give, we once again learned the significance of receiving.

Arohanui New Zealand—we will always love you and yours.

Bart and Bret getting ready to perform a huka.

Maroi Culture
Utah Visit 2009

Mark, Karewa,
Sonny, & Brian.

Hangai Christmas,
1978

Chris & Karewa
Arthur and family.

Tim & Helen Beaglehole
with family.

Rangi & Vic Parker

Beau Moller Family

Karewa Arthur Family

Kay with the
Sydney Opera
House in the
background.

Matt and
Japanese tourists,
Christchurch, NZ

Ross and Karewa Arthur
D'Urville Island, NZ

Ross and Kay, 1987
Editors, *Dialogue*

HECTIC HOLIDAY: CHRISTMAS IN SALT LAKE CITY
Written 2023

December blizzards in the Rocky Mountains are to be expected. In a small village or even a college town like Logan, you stay put and ride them out. A windswept horizontal snowfall in Salt Lake City or Denver is different. Christmas urban traffic compounds the mess. People are inclined to still try to make their way to a planned event, like seeing lights all over Temple Square or a Utah Jazz game, so driving is chaotic. Snowplows stick to the main streets or highways and neighborhood roads are left to accumulate.

A particularly nasty storm swept through Salt Lake City in mid-December of 1988. I slowly drove south from the University of Utah campus after turning in my grades to the History Department. I picked Ninth East and drove slowly, plowing snow with our 1983 Plymouth eleven-passenger van. The windswept snow was pelting the right side of the van as growing drifts impeded my progress toward our rented home near Forty-fifth South. Our family planned on gathering for Christmas in the next few days by driving from Phoenix, flying from North Carolina and Washington, D.C., and some coming down from Logan.

Our youngest son, Fred (Matthew), and I were not happy about being in Salt Lake for Christmas. In fact, eleven-year-old Fred was not amused to be in Salt Lake at all. My second sabbatical from Utah State dictated that I remain close to Utah. The first sabbatical was to New Zealand with a Fulbright Fellowship and Fred was one year old, with no memory of even a day of that wonderful experience.

When I announced that we were going to Salt Lake City for a school year, his sixth grade, he offered to resign from the family and join the family of his friends, the Budges. He had finally reached the epitome of elementary school power as a sixth grader in River Heights. Now he was going to Dilworth Elementary, a gigantic school on Twenty-first East in Salt Lake. Bret and Julie had moved to the Phoenix area after he graduated from USU, and Bart was in his second year at Guilford College in North Carolina. So, it was a disgruntled Fred and us.

There were three reasons I had to stay near Utah's Capital City. I had postponed applying for a sabbatical because of a series of commitments. In 1986, Glenn R. Wilde and I authored a proposal to establish the Mountain West Center for Regional Studies at Utah State University that was funded by the National

Endowment for the Humanities. We received a Challenge Grant that committed us to raise 1.2 million dollars and the NEH will give $400,000. I resigned as department Head and assumed the title of Director of the Center.

Secondly, I had been appointed to the Utah Endowment for the Humanities (later the Utah Humanities Council), a six-year commitment. I became the Acting Chair in 1988 when my predecessor went to Japan for her child's educational experience.

Finally, in 1987, after six months of intense recruiting by many academic friends, Kay and I accepted the editorship of Dialogue, A Journal of Mormon Thought, a five-year commitment. Since the UEH and Dialogue were officed in Salt Lake City and philanthropic foundations and individuals were more plentiful there, we chose to move eighty miles south.

There were two major obstacles facing us. One, we needed to rent our house, and two, we needed to find a house to rent. This led to my initial major mistake which totally created a lack of domestic tranquility and trust. When one of my students, Tim Moran, offered to stay in the house and find four others, maybe five, perhaps at times, six cohorts to share, I said "Sure."

Kay was less than amused and although she loved Tim, domestic cleanliness is usually not associated with a house of young men. I argued that most apartment owners in Logan preferred young men to coeds for obvious reasons. The first was less hair, second, fewer appliances, third, men had less magnetic properties. In other words, girls' apartments drew men like honey does flies. Kay, in very sharp tones, called my argument for what it was—pure Baloney. However, she acquiesced to my promise, and I have lived with the consequences for nearly four decades.

Our Salt Lake City search for a home and for additional resources was solved by two owners of the famous Alexander Cartwright Fantasy Baseball League. Founded in 1977, the franchises were owned by historians of baseball and fans in the Salt Lake area. Craig Fuller of the Cache Valley Trappers and an executive of the Utah Historical Society informed us that a couple in his ward had accepted a mission call and wanted someone to rent their furnished home. I think the price including utilities amounted to $200 a month. The home was located within ten minutes of the University of Utah, downtown, and Dilworth Elementary. Larry Gerlach, the History Department head, as well as owner of the Yankee Doodles, offered me a class to teach fall and winter quarters.

However, he requested the third-round draft pick of the Bear Lake Monsters in return. I argued against this as a violation of church-state relations, but he countered that although baseball certainly had a religious component to some fans, it would never stand up in court. I relented. Jack Newell, the previous editor of *Dialogue* (with his wife, Linda), offered me a class for spring quarter in Liberal Studies, so all rent and utilities were in the bank.

There was no doubt we were busy and often stressed. However, we expanded our circle of friends dramatically. Obert C. Tanner had always been a supporter of the Humanities and *Dialogue*. I loved going to his office on South State Street and having lunch with him and some of his friends in the small cafeteria with a retractable roof. As a leading Utah philanthropist, he cared deeply about cultural expansion. Once he had confidence in me as an independent thinker, he carefully chose to support our causes on his own terms. However, it came with a commitment by me to help him get two manuscripts ready for publication. *One Man's Search* is a compilation of his essays on various topics and *One Man's Journey* is his autobiography.

Obert Tanner enjoyed giving and he taught me the art of philanthropy through trust in relationships and patience. On the other hand, I watched him solve problems among competing grant requesters. He called a donation that he gave the Utah Symphony and the Mormon Tabernacle choir, "The Gift of Music." Originally, he stipulated that the two organizations had to perform a joint concert once a year.

By November, we had a routine established that created degrees of peace and success on all fronts. We accepted an invitation to fly to Texas for Thanksgiving with our longtime friends. Otto and Wanda Puempel. We arranged to have Bart fly in from Greensboro and made arrangements to all arrive on Tuesday. As a gift to the Puempels, I offered to get tickets for the annual Dallas Cowboy Thanksgiving Day football game at Texas Stadium in Irving. This meant that all plans for the dinner had to be changed because the game was in the afternoon on the actual holiday. Everyone did a count of who wanted to go and suddenly there was a need for twelve tickets. While youngsters were placing bets on whether I could accumulate that many tickets, I went to work and played two aces quickly and held a third in reserve.

The Cowboys were slated to play the Houston Oilers and two of my former students, Al Smith and Patrick" Doc" Allen, were members of the Oilers. If they could not deliver, a third Aggie alum, Cornell Green, was a scout for the Cowboys. He was a year ahead of me in school, but I had re-connected with him when we lived in Arlington, Texas. I never had to play the Cornell ace; the other two came through and informed me that I had to get the tickets directly from them the night before the game at their hotel near the airport.

On Wednesday, Bart and I drove to Waco with Otto. He had opened an additional medical office there. We teased Otto about becoming a chain, and then borrowed his car to drive to Austin where I spent most of the day researching in the Johnson Presidential Library.

Later we drove back to Waco and picked up Otto. Interstate 35 was impossible. Students from both Texas A&M and UT Austin, on Thanksgiving break, were traveling north to the Dallas-Fort Worth area. We decided to go directly to the hotel to get the tickets prior to the curfew. We barely made it and in the days before cell phones instant communication did not exist, so it was nearly ten when we hit the front desk and tried to get Al and Doc's room numbers. The clerk was finally persuaded to call the rooms and make contact for us. We went to Al's room which he shared with Curtis Duncan and then he called Doc who came out and met us. We were not invited in as Doc said that Jackie Sherrill's "gifts" were in the room and that they were "not alone." Bart had to explain all of this to me. We got our twelve tickets and the next day, the Cowboys gifted the Oilers a fairly boring game: a 25-17 loss with five field goals.

The Christmas season was in full force in Texas as we all finally sat down together on Saturday. Bart sent Fred into a major emotional funk when he announced that he was leaving

Guilford and transferring to BYU. Guilford had gone from NAIA to Division 3 of the NCAA which meant the school no longer offered athletic scholarships. For Fred, and most of us, Bart at BYU was totally unimaginable. It had nothing to do with baseball, it simply violated a fundamental Peterson religious tenant, "Nothing good ever came from Provo." Fred fumed back to Utah.

While in Texas, we called Kay's brother and his family, their mother, and all of my siblings and invited them to gather for Christmas events in Salt Lake. We had plenty of room in the Richard and Fern Muir home for a large crowd. Everyone seemed excited to have a different experience. When we got back to Salt Lake late Sunday night, Craig Fuller was waiting for us.

"Dick Muir had a stroke in Massachusetts and they are coming home as soon as he can travel. Fern said if you cannot find another place, they will find something with their family."

"We'll see what we can do," I said. "They need to be in their home."

Our first option was to assemble members of the Aggie SLC Mafia. I called Doug Foxley on Monday morning and we agreed to meet after my class at Dan Jones's office on Seventh East. Kay and I agreed that everyone could change their Christmas plans, but some had already bought tickets.

The snow was coming down again as I approached Dan's office. Doug worked for the

Governor and was starting a lobbyist firm and Dan was Utah's leading pollster. They had both just knocked homeruns in the 1988 election and probably had a few "debts" to collect. We called Dave Johnson, who was married to Kay's cousin, Kim. He was also plugged into real estate in SLC.

After I explained our plight and we discussed some ideas and contacts, Pat Jones, Dan's wife, walked in, listened, and left. A few minutes later, with no results from our brain trust, Pat came back and announced. "Merry Christmas, I have a place for you and Kay-my parents said you could live in their house until you leave!" Her parents, Harley and Lucille Workman, owned a motor home and had planned to leave after Christmas on a trip to wherever it was warm. Harley, a retired railroad engineer and World War II veteran, thought traveling around the country all winter was a great adventure.

Thanksgiving in Texas had been a gift, but the Workman home was icing on the cake. No plans had to be changed. In seventy two hours our dilemma was solved and we moved from the Muir's home to the Workman's home. The new house was a little smaller and about three miles farther south. The only problem was the length of commute for Fred to Dilworth, Kay to the *Dialogue* office, and me to the University of Utah.

Ironically, the experience with the homes prepared us for another major decision. Allen Roberts, one of the architects who owned the building where *Dialogue* was housed, informed us that the firm had to hire some more architects and we had to move the journal. Within hours, Ron Molen, another architect, invited us to set up temporary offices in his building on 600 East, so we moved quickly and efficiently. It also prompted us to realize that we just as well take the operation to Logan for the next three years and USU provided space. There is never a need to panic when you have a network of friends.

I am not sure if Doug, Dan, Dave, or Theron Godfrey conspired to make sure that we had tickets to Jazz games, but that certainly made Fred's stay much easier. The Christmas season in Salt Lake enabled us to experience different types of celebrations in person. The Humanities group gave us access to many programs we sponsored, *Dialogue* had a large contingent of Christmas activities, and many of the Salt Lake crowd helped us raise money for the Mountain West Center. In fact, one visit with the Freed family encouraged them to give an amazing collection of photographs to USU's Special collection that were evaluated at over a quarter of a million dollars.

Leonard Arrington, the LDS Church Historian at the time introduced me to the Evans family who transferred an annual biography award to

USU. He also helped the Preston Nibley and Conway Sonne families endow scholarships and the heavy weight of being a novice in the fundraising world disappeared as the match was met nearly a year early.

The gift to be together and provide a place where many could stay made memories. Kay's mother, Geanie, spent the holidays with us and the Workman home proved to be a haven and a magnet. Bret and Julie came from Phoenix and moved back and forth from Logan and her family. Bart made the transition to Provo and got set up for baseball and school. Larry and Peggi came from Virginia with their five sons and those who wanted to try skiing had a great time. They all enjoyed concerts at the Tabernacle on Temple Square as well as touring groups like Mannheim Steamroller. Kay took some to the Nutcracker Ballet. People rotated in and out of the house with ease and if they helped change the sheets, sat down to use the bathroom, and not leave essential items when they left, life was great.

Shortly after Christmas, I was driving along South Temple headed to the *Dialogue* office. There was a young man, fairly disheveled, walking on the right hand side of the road and as I passed by, I thought I recognized him. Quickly pulling over in our large van, I opened the passenger door and asked if I could give him a ride. It was cold and January can be bitter, so he slowly got into the van, but kept his head turned slightly. As I always do, I try to connect with any person by a geographical and genealogical check-where is he from and who is he related to. He was hesitant to engage or reveal, but finally said, "You taught me up at USU."

"When?"

"Oh, about ten years ago."

Then he filled in the blanks. He had gotten married, had two children, stopped going to school for a job, had been laid off and after six months of being out of work, he and his wife, made difficult decisions. They divorced in order for her to get maximum benefits from unemployment and family assistance programs. He stayed close and tried to get on top of some sort of job. This winter had been bad, and he was going to the Homeless Shelter and St. Paul's on Fourth West and Second South.

I offered to buy him lunch and pulled into the JB's on South Temple. I tried to visit, but he had a heavy shield around him. Unable to penetrate for a name, hometown, or family connections, I resorted to discussing assistance programs. His family was near her parents and the children were doing OK, but in his mind, he was failing. After giving him a little money, I dropped him off on the west side and gave him a card with my information. This too, is a lasting memory of the Christmas season in Salt Lake City.

When I think back on those six years of so many demands on time and energy, I realize that even though mistakes were made, commitments were kept. Everyone one of the groups that asked us to accept a position of leadership taught me about caring for others. We hoped that *Dialogue*, the UEH, and the Mountain West Center were a bit better after we moved on to other opportunities.

It was an exhausting but rewarding time, in part because Christmas became the focal point of our time away. The breadth of friendships became an important reality and source of support. In every challenge, we tried to follow the admonition of Jesus in Matthew 25 and with that as a guide, our eyes remained focused on what is good for all of God's children.

Ross and Kay

Texas Stadium, Thanksgiving 1988

Kay and Lisa Watson,
Smithsonian Sunstone 1990

Kay and Linda Newell

Linda & Jack Newell

Swinging T entrance.

"HOLIDAY INN" at DEEP SPRINGS

Written 2011

This is a true story. The names have not been changed because no one is innocent. It is a tale of some degree of anxiety, but is a reminder that Christmas began when travelers found refuge in a stable. Two thousand years later, we are still given opportunity to share and care, even in an isolated desert valley.

Kay and I looked forward with great anticipation to our first Christmas as President and First Lady of Deep Springs College, a tiny school with 26 remarkable male students. Between Christmas 2004 and early January 2005, Deep Springs (DS) experienced an amazing adventure which epitomized the true spirit of Christmas. This time of year in Deep Springs Valley is ordinarily a time of quiet, dry solitude.

At 5200' elevation, the high desert valley is isolated from the rest of the Eastern Sierra Nevada world. California State Highway 168 slices through the valley from Nevada's highway 266 to California's US 395. Gilbert Pass (6400') moves travelers from Nevada's Fish Lake Valley into Deep Springs Valley from the northeast. These same travelers leave DS to the northwest via Westgard Pass (7200') into California's Owens Valley.

Christmas break at Deep Springs College means that most students and faculty leave the valley, but because the college is also a working cattle ranch, some must stay to milk cows, feed cattle, horses, pigs and chickens, cook meals and clean up after each other. December also begins the calving season for the new heifers.

In 2004, this meant that Ranch Managers Geoff and Iris Pope and student cowboys Gareth and Mitch were on constant watch to assist in the births and then to shelter the newborns from the biting wind and freezing temperatures. By the end of December, 32 of 45 heifers had calved and then snow began to fall throughout Deep Springs Valley. Because the valley is in the shadow of the majestic snow-hogging Sierras, vast amounts of snow do not normally accumulate; however, within a few days this season, over three feet of snow lay on the valley floor.

There were six students in residence at the college as well as two young lady friends. Also in residence were the full staff, former DS President Jack and Linda Newell (visiting for a week of research for their history of DS project), and visiting professor Robley Williams. Jack and I had just shoveled all the snow off several flat-roofed buildings when the phone rang in our house. My brother Brent in Los Angeles was on the line.

"They canceled that flight to Israel and Noah and Sam are here wondering what to do."

Three Jewish students—Noah B, Sam and Sean—had signed up to go on a privately-sponsored tour of Israel. Noah and Sam were flying out of Los Angeles and Sean was to meet them in Israel. Noah claimed it was a "matchmaking" group who tried to preserve Jewish culture by providing an opportunity for young Americans to share the experience of the homeland. The LA-based airplane's departure had been postponed for three consecutive days because of mechanical difficulties and weather. The two Deep Springers decided to return to the college rather than wait any longer for another flight.

I asked my brother to let them stay a night with them and by morning they could drive the five hours north back to Deep Springs before the next storm.

"There are three of them.

"What do you mean?" I asked. "Is Sean with them?"

"No, it is a she."

"Oh man, we do not need another 'friend-of-the-family' here right now:

"What should I tell them?

I thought, "Let me talk to Sam."

Sam said very properly, "Hello, Dr. Peterson."

Deep Springs is the most informal place in the world. Twenty-five students called us Ross and Kay. Sam, preparing for an educational transfer to Oxford University in England, never allowed himself that luxury.

"Sam, you and Noah hustle up here in the morning. There is a lot of snow and we need to get you home before we get any more."

"Well," I'd like to bring our new friend for a few days."

"How will she get home?"

"Ummm, she goes to Berkeley and she'll find a way."

A little more forcefully, "Sam, it will be much easier if you have Brent put her on a plane to the Bay area tomorrow and you and Noah can hit the road, OK?"

"Alright."

At 1:00 p.m. the next day, the three of them drove into the valley. Sam had the great talent of looking me right in the eye and then doing the exact thing that I had asked him not to do. One more female friend was now in the valley.

That afternoon, ominous skies brought more snow accompanied by howling winds which quickly became a primary factor in "life in the valley." As the snow intensified, Mike Bodine, DS cook, became nervous about the weather and left early from the college for his family home in Bishop. This left long term faculty members Ellie and Gary Gossen to finish his job of cooking for the community. Mike made it safely the 27 miles over the high mountain Westgard Pass to Big Pine, but it took him one and one-half hours to drive the remaining 15 miles to Bishop.

Earlier that morning, our Maintenance Supervisor Les Smith and Gareth drove the DS Suburban over Westgard Pass to Bishop for the weekly driver's trip to pick up supplies for the college. Les was also to retrieve his wife, Debbie, and their Blazer, stranded in the Owens Valley due to the extreme weather conditions. The two vehicles drove in tandem on their return trip to DS in the early afternoon. Part way up the steep climb up Westgard, the Smith's Blazer spun-out into a snow bank. Gareth, in the Suburban, turned around to assist them, and in the process an axle broke on that vehicle.

By the time Les and Gareth transferred all the school's supplies into the Blazer, road conditions had deteriorated to the point that they could not handle the steep grade. Fortunately, they were still on the Owens Valley side of the mountain where cell phones worked. They called a tow truck from Bishop to pick up the Suburban and Geoff Pope at the ranch for help. Geoff and student Derek left about 4:30 p.m. for the rescue in Geoff's Tahoe. Darkness was rapidly approaching and all available snowplows were occupied on US 395.

In the meantime, the Post-Mistress of the Dyer, Nevada Post Office called DS to check on David Carro, our remarkable mailman (and a proud Paiute Indian who did not seem to own long pants, or at least never wore them). David covered nearly three hundred rural miles daily and now he was over two hours late to DS with the storm intensifying by the minute.

At the same time that Geoff and Derek were heading west over Westgard Pass to rescue the Smith's and Gareth, Farm Manager Ken Mitchell, Jack Newell and I drove east toward Gilbert Pass to look for our missing mailman. Rounding a sharp curve half-way up the mountain, we came across a small Honda station wagon which had slid off the road. Huddled in the car were four Korean college students while a fifth was standing on a snow drift trying in vain to call OnStar for help. Cell phones never worked in the valley and our land-line phone system was irregular, at best.

The car was so buried and high-centered that it could not be pulled out. After assuring the five frightened students that we would return for them, we continued up the pass searching for David Carro. A mile up the road, huge drifts forced us to turn around. We loaded the Korean students (two male and three female) and their belongings into our truck, arriving at the Boarding House (BH) about 6:30 p.m.

Following dinner, our new guests were "settled" into the two Withrow guest cottages. By then, we learned that these students had gone to Mammoth to ski but the great amount of snow kept them off the slopes. They decided to go to Las Vegas to gamble instead and chose the Hwy 168 cutoff through DS valley to get there (a decision they were now questioning!).

Kay received a phone call with the welcome news that the Esmeralda County Deputies had found mailman David stuck in a five-foot snow drift, rescued him and his little green truck and took them back to Dyer.

Back up on Westgard Pass, Geoff and Derek made it through to Les, Debbie and Gareth. They successfully pulled them out and actually towed them all the way up and over the pass to DS in a raging blizzard. They drove into the Main Circle about 8:30 p.m. The community discussed their high adventures, visited late into the night and retired after an exhausting day.

Near midnight, I received another phone call. A knock at Les and Debbie's door at the Maintenance Station on Highway 168 had brought four male Cal State Fullerton students asking for assistance. They had also been snowed out at Mammoth and decided to seek the pleasures of Las Vegas. Finding Gilbert impassable, they fortunately avoided becoming hopelessly stuck and were able to drive back down to the valley. Shortly after 1:00 a.m., the DS students put them in the Rumpus Room in the Dorm; and then the snow really hit. California Transportation (CalTrans) called and said Highway 168 was officially closed from both ends.

There was one other serious problem. Saturday was the day we were supposed to pick up the students returning from Christmas break. Three were flying into Los Angeles to connect with our LA student, Bryce, who was going to drive them back to DS with him. The other fourteen were coming through Las Vegas. We could not get out of the valley to retrieve them and the Greyhound bus no longer ran between Las Vegas and Reno. Historically, DS students took the bus from Las Vegas to the junction of Nevada Hwy 266 and US 95 at the "Cottontail Ranch" (there were neither cottontails nor was it a "ranch") where our van would pick them up for a one-hour ride to the college. Unfortunately, the bus was no longer an option.

Noah R. called all of those students with cell phones to tell them to stay in Las Vegas until they heard from us. DS students always used a code to gather at the LV McCarran airport. One would call on the white courtesy phone to have the PA announcer ask that "L.L. Nunn, please go to the baggage claim!"

Nunn was the founder of Deep Springs College (in 1917) and everyone got the drift. I coordinated their return flights so that they all arrived within an hour or two of each other. We would then normally pick them up in the DS fifteen passenger Dodge van at a prearranged spot in short-term parking.

By mid afternoon on Saturday, thirteen of the fourteen had reported in and were told to "occupy McCarran." Sean then notified us that he would not get there until Tuesday. He had his own car and always came and left at break on his own schedule.

Throughout Saturday, CalTrans assessed the situation and chose to try to open Westgard Pass. At the college, our students and the Fullerton students pitched in on labor in a major way and a semi-festive atmosphere pervaded in the valley.

That night, popcorn was popped and our new projector inaugurated with "Seven Brides for Seven Brothers" shown in the Main Room. The six young women were not amused as the avalanche scene sealed the kidnapped potential brides in a mountain enclave. Two of the Korean girls actually began to cry. However, the math did not add up, so the movie caused no incidents of bridal capture.

Sunday morning, following CalTrans' success in plowing through Westgard Pass, Ken Mitchell and I decided to make a break out of the valley to retrieve the returning students from Las Vegas. (There had been no success in cutting through Gilbert Pass and it was still closed for the foreseeable future.) The roads remained too hazardous for the van, so we each prepared to take our personal four-wheel-drive vehicles. Already delayed a day because of weather, a caravan of four cars-Ken and I (with the three female friends), Jack and Linda Newell, and the four Fullerton State students-drove out Westgard just after 8:00 a.m. for our various destinations. A CalTrans vehicle led us through the "narrows," a one-lane section of the pass. The roads were not good, but passable.

The Fullerton students turned south at Big Pine and left for home. We stopped and bade farewell to the Newells who were heading north at Tonapah. After listening to the "friends" discuss the adventure, I told Ken, "There is no romance left in that group."

Kay and Iris Pope manned a command center at Deep Springs, fielding calls from CalTrans, Nevada Department of Transportation, 26 sets of parents and many students. A call from CalTrans to the college shortly after the caravan had made its way through Westgard informed them that an avalanche in the narrows had closed the road until further notice. Geoff immediately notified all callers to "stay put" until they heard from the college.

Before we left Tonapah, we called the students in Las Vegas and told them to be at the parking terrace at 2:00 p.m. Some of them had gone to a motel and others had just slept at the airport. Then, just as we drove into LV, Iris called with the CalTrans news of the avalanche. Uncertain now, Ken and I decided to go back as far as Beatty, NV, Gateway to Death Valley, rather than spend any more time in LV. As a precaution, I asked Kay and Iris to reserve four rooms for fifteen people at Motel 6 in Beatty, two and one-half hours closer to DS. The students were ready to get back to school and they just wanted to sleep.

We loaded all of their bags into the two SUVs. Every seat was taken and every square inch filled with luggage. Then Isak appeared with a full-sized snowboard. This was the same student who had arrived at DS in the fall with a very large Kayak. Deep Springs is in a land-locked high desert valley with one tiny stream and nowhere to snowboard.

"Isak! Why? There is no room-no room!" I yelled.

"Well, he replied quietly, "I thought we might go to Mammoth." Isak always spoke softly and I had long ago given up trying to understand exactly where his thought processes touched reality.

"Isak, you are killing me." He knew I would not leave him or the snowboard.

Julian suggested putting all of the smaller-butt people in the Durango and the larger endowed in Ken's Suburban. It was the only time we divided the students based on butt-width. The snowboard and Isak ended up in the Durango with five other students and me. Beatty was our destination that evening.

Suddenly, Matt growled, "Lane, why are you in the front seat?" Lane was short, but not thin. His legs and body deserved row two, but he had somehow nabbed the "shotgun." He feigned sleep and did not respond. Matt grumbled for awhile but soon fell asleep.

Further to the west in L.A., the four DS students had congregated at the home of Bryce beginning on Friday and had been stranded there because of the snowy conditions at DS followed by torrential rain in the Los Angeles area. Also stranded in L.A. were incoming short-term faculty members from Denmark, Misha and Anna Hoekstra and baby Esther. Just as the DS command post determined to finally give them the go-ahead to drive to the college, they were notified of the avalanche.

Now stranded outside the valley were 17 students, Ross and Ken, incoming short-term faculty, Fred and Julie Will of Iowa (who had already been detained because of weather, first in Flagstaff, then in Beatty, and now in Bishop), the Hoekstra's, Professors David Arndt and Julie Park, Asst-to-the Pres Diane Seidenverg and DS cook Mike Bodine. Stranded inside the valley were Kay, the Popes, Gossens, Smiths, five members of the Mitchell family, eight DS students and the five Korean students because their car remained buried on Gilbert Pass.

Frustrated by the road closure at Big Pine, David Arndt and Julie Park drove up the mountain to see the slide for themselves. They (and their two little yappy dogs) had lived their entire married lives at Deep Springs as long term professors. Julie convinced David they could get through the avalanche.

When the snow removal crew stopped them, Julie jumped from the car (no winter coat or boots on), climbed up the snow bank and crawled her way to the other side of the slide. The CalTrans workers and David screamed at her, but she just kept going.

David turned his car around and raced back to Big Pine to call the college. He asked for students Gareth and Mitch, who, without telling Geoff, took off in one of the ranch trucks to find Julie. They battled the perilous road conditions and finally found her trudging toward Deep Springs. When they entered the BH two hours later, Julie announced her entrance with a bow and a cheesy smile.

Ellie Gossen, highly educated and quite refined, rose quickly and verbally undressed and exposed Julie in words that would make any mule skinner envious. Geoff and Iris called the young rescuers to task for not clearing with them before they ventured out for their mission.

In the meantime, Ken, Ross and the students arrived in Beatty where they spent the night. Monday they made their way back through Tonapah over Montgomery Pass on Highway 6 into Bishop. Kay called with word that CalTrans would escort a group of DS vehicles through the pass. So, the Wills, David Arndt, Ross and Ken met the CalTrans guide at the "Road Closed" barricade at Big Pine at 3:00 p.m. for the trip back into the valley.

Just in time, Geoff, Les and the two male Korean students received word that the roadway had been cleared up to the stranded car on Gilbert and they successfully retrieved it from its three-day snow cave. The CalTrans driver guided our group into the valley and led our stranded visitors out on his return trip.

The LA contingent still could not leave because of continued torrential rain and flooding. Ross arranged for Bryce's parents, Diana and Richard Goodman, to fly the LA group to Las Vegas so they could connect with Sean, the last returning student, arriving via NYC after his break visit to Israel. Arriving about Midnight, Sean-totally unaware that three students needed his shuttle service because he was flying and could not be reached by phone-was met by Tom, Beau, and J (the McCarran "L.L. Nunn" code worked!).

They drove to Beatty for the rest of their short night. We had every hope that Sean's vehicle would be able to make it over Lida Pass and Gilbert on Tuesday morning. However, this was not to be and they had to retreat back down Gilbert to the Esmeralda Market in Dyer where they called DS for help. Ken picked them up in the ranch truck and they had to leave Sean's car at Diane's home in Fish Lake Valley.

Misha and Anna Hoekstra, the final stragglers for Term 4 came in at 10:30 p.m. Tuesday from a sunny LA. They proved to be the only returnees who did not have to be "rescued" in order to get to DS. A sudden turn-of-events left Bryce in LA for gall bladder surgery scheduled for a week later.

Classes for Term 4 were postponed from Monday until Wednesday. So, other than that, it was just another typical week at Deep Springs College. We were extremely grateful for the "extreme adventure" of DS living and especially for the safe return of all community members that winter season.

As citizens of the Deep Springs community, we had a wonderful, meaningful Christmas. The isolation, combined with heavy snowfall and blizzard conditions, created a complete necessity for service. We provided food and shelter for the frightened travelers, rescued those who found themselves separated from where they needed to be, and lived the spirit of the season.

Most significantly, we witnessed an absolute miracle in that the antiquated microwave DS phone system worked beautifully throughout the storm and during the complicated process of bringing everyone back to the valley. Once we all nestled into the peaceful comfort of safety, the phones were totally out for over a week.

The night after Ken Mitchell brought the last four students into the valley, I chopped some wood and built a nice fire in our fireplace. Pulling the big chair close, put my feet up on the coffee table, and breathed a sign of relief. I actually thought of turning off the porch light, a signal that visitors were not welcome. There was a knock on the door and before I could yell, "Come In!" the door opened. Mitch and Isak appeared, took off their boots and moved to my side at the fire.

Isak began quietly, but grew animated as he described a series of communiques with the owner of a river-running company in Colorado. It seems Isak had arranged for the DS Student Body (SB) during their Spring break to help the man prepare his camp and rafts for the summer. As payment, the guide would take them on the first run of the season down the Green River of Utah. Mitch just sat there and rolled his eyes.

"We could help them get the gear ready and they would take us down the river-just to try everything out!"

"Isak, stop! You are killing me!"

L.L. Nunn said the purpose of Deep Springs is to prepare young men for lives of service to humanity. Bright minds never stop; thus, no two days are the same at Deep Springs. It is a unique community and Christmas in some form happens every day.

*DS students identified by first names only

* Twenty-two of the twenty-six DS students completed the trip to Colorado, floated the Green River and ALL survived! The Green River is VERY cold in March.

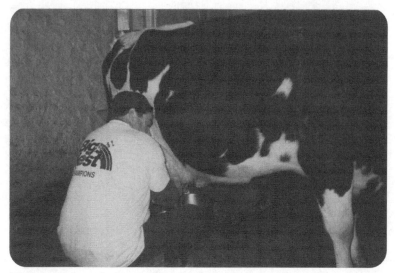

Ross milking during a storm.

Gift from a student at Deep
Springs to Ross.

Ellie Gossen in the midst
of a storm

Ross shoveling snow in front of Aird Cottage.

Korean students
at Deep Springs.

Kay, Sierra ride, 2005

Row: Jake Sweet, Cade Puempel, Andi Puempel, Hazel Puempel, Kate Peterson, Rose Godfrey, Aliya Peterson, Jack Godfrey, Anthony Peterson, Gavin Peterson

Row 2: Erin Peterson, Kylee Peterson, Bailey Peterson, Conner Johnson, Blake Puempel, Brooke Peterson, Jamie Peterson (holding Molly Peterson), Max Sweet

Row 3: Carly Oldroyd, Abby Oldroyd, McKenzie, Otto Puempel, Wanda Puempel, Ross, Brandon Peterson, Cole Godfrey, Carson Johnson

Rows 4-5: Todd Puempel, Taylor Johnson, Chris Puempel, Mike sweet, Amy Johnson, Christy Oldroyd, Mark Johnson, Brad Oldroyd, Jay Puempel, Dorothy Puempel, Bart Peterson, Jen Peterson, Kay, Kami Peterson, Red Peterson, Julie Peterson, Bret Peterson, Lisa Godfrey, LJ Godfrey, Noralyn Peterson, Tyrasha Peterson, Brent Peterson, Noraina Peterson

A CHRISTMAS LIKE NO OTHER
"TAKE ME OUT TO THE BALLGAME"

Written 2021

The sun had barely begun to rise as we turned east from the Deep Springs Road onto CA Hwy 168 for Christmas break and our home in Logan, Utah. It was the shortest day of the year, and with no snow forecast across Nevada, we could make good time. After a gasoline stop in Ely, NV, we began a conversation about our Christmas plans. I randomly mentioned that I had not written an annual Christmas story for our family. Oh, oh! This was serious business!

Six hours later, following intense discussion, compromise, and brainstorming, we finalized an agreement on a new Christmas concept. We decided to forego the traditional gift-giving and make this Christmas a "Living Christmas Story." The proposal was to bring our three son's families together the following summer (2007) and share a ten-day Bus Tour in the Eastern United States. Thanks to our "nest egg" tucked away in an account at Cache Valley Bank, the Tour would be our Christmas gift to the family.

For the previous three years, we had lived at Deep Springs College in California causing us to be mostly absent from our children's and grandchildren's lives. The dance reviews, ballgames, soccer matches, school honors, etc. had been enjoyed vicariously. We loved the position as President of Deep Springs and considered staying on for another term. But for our grandchildren, all living in Utah, that idea did not generate enthusiasm. During a summer visit, one of them, Anthony, bluntly told us "We need you more than these boys."

That fall, my long-time friend, Stan Albrecht, now the President of Utah State University, had a different plan for me. He asked me to come back to Logan, Utah as Vice President for Advancement at our alma mater. After outlining his specific goals for a comprehensive capital campaign, I agreed to return to Utah State. Kay and I prepared to leave Deep Springs at the end of the school year in June 2007.

During our official meeting held in the Durango, we prepared an itinerary to present at our traditional family gathering on Christmas Eve. As we drove across the Salt Flats toward Salt Lake City, we thought of how to approach the children, give them potential dates, and explain that attendance of every family member was our greatest desire.

Our family gathered on Christmas Eve day, had a nice meal, read my new Christmas story, and exchanged gifts before they left for other activities. When we arrived in Logan, we got some food, put up a small tree, and prepared for the Christmas Eve gathering. Kay wondered, "How do you think they will respond?"

Our family in 2006, consisted of the three sons (Bret, Bart, and Fred), their wives (Julie, Jen, and Kami), eight granddaughters between the ages of thirteen years and a three-month-old baby, three grandsons, between sixteen and five years and the two of us adding up to nineteen. They enjoyed the Christmas stories which had been written every year since 1999 and were given to each family at our Christmas party.

As soon as we fed everyone and gathered in our living room, I announced there was not a story this year. They looked confused until Kay passed out the itinerary of a bus tour beginning in Baltimore, to Philadelphia, to Gettysburg, and back to Washington, D.C. Then up to New York, to Cooperstown and the Baseball Hall of Fame, Springfield, Massachusetts, and the Basketball Hall of Fame, and ending at Fenway Park in Boston. It was to be a combined History, Culture, and Baseball agenda which included a Broadway musical, major league games in every city (if the team was at home), all Smithsonian Museums, National Battlefields, monuments, and other sites. The proposal was to be ten days on the road in a large luxury coach (not a yellow school bus).

"This is our Christmas gift, and we want everyone to go," Kay proclaimed.

After checking various schedules, we agreed on the last week of July into the first week of August. "Please plan for those days and we will work out the details. Let us know of anything that you really want to see in any of the cities," I explained.

As we discussed the idea everyone seemed enthused and excited as we told them again, "This is our 2006 Christmas gift to you." Now that the gift had been revealed, we added another proposal—we needed to fill the big bus. I explained, "The bus usually carries between forty-five to fifty people." Everyone agreed that we should invite any family members and friends who might be interested.

Kay and I had led six Alumni Tours for Utah State University and knew how to maneuver from venue to venue, site to site, and city to city. We had been everywhere on the proposed tour except Cooperstown, NY and Springfield, MA. Kay and I decided to use the advice of a travel agent, Teneale Hollingshead, in Logan, to help us find the bus, book the hotels, and work out the airfare. We agreed to handle the tickets to ballgames, a Broadway musical, museums, and historical parks.

Our plan included taking full advantage of the National Park Service's many venues. Teneale worked at pricing everything, so our additional guests knew the cost far in advance. We covered all of this with the family, spent Christmas in Utah, and left on Boxing Day (December 26) to return to our California College.

Once back at Deep Springs, Kay sent out an invitation to our siblings about the trip asking them to consider joining us. For most, the middle of the summer was not a good time for a variety of reasons. However, my brother, Brent and wife Noralyn and Kay's brother, Larry and wife Peggi jumped at the chance. We now had twenty-five in the fold.

Our sons suggested we ask our long-time friends from Texas, Otto and Wanda Puempel, and their children. By early February, 19 of their family had signed on. In our obsession to create an opportunity, I sent out a note to many friends saying, "First nine who respond have the trip of a lifetime." Within hours, two families of great friends responded—L.J. and Lisa Godfrey (5) and Brad and Christy Oldroyd (4). The bus was now completely full at 54, (counting Molly, ten months) the dates were set, and the logistics gradually fell into place.

Kay and Teneale finalized transportation with the Hood Valley Line out of Baltimore, housing through the Hilton Chain, and appointments at Museums and Parks. According to the bus company, when their drivers saw the agenda, every one of them volunteered for the trip. However, when they saw the ages of the travelers (seventeen girls under eighteen and a dozen boys the same age) only one driver, Robert Bradley, stayed the course. Drivers make all the difference on a bus tour and Big Bob Bradley was "King of the Road." It helped that he had eight children of his own and bonded with the youngsters. My assignment was obtaining tickets for the three baseball games, two Halls of Fame, and a Broadway Musical.

Deep Springs never had reliable phone service—landline or cell—which was necessary for negotiations with the Yankees, Orioles, and Phillies. (The Nationals and Red Sox were not at home during the days we would be there.) We also needed a personal touch with the Broadway Theatre's offices as well. Since cell phones did not work in Deep Springs Valley, anytime I had to travel to Bishop, CA for any reason, I left at 4:30 a.m., stopped in Big Pine, sat at a table outside the Chevron station and used my cell phone.

As offices opened on the east coast, mine was the first call. Twice the local Big Pine constable "grilled me" as to my intent. After I explained to the officer that there was no phone service at Deep Springs, we had a huge family trip to plan, and I wanted my call to be the first of the day in the eastern time zone, he wandered off shaking his head. I needed more time to tell the story of why we were doing this journey—all about Family, Christmas, Community and Country.

Throughout the winter and spring of 2007, we worked hard to finish our three-year stint at Deep Springs with devotion and attention. The second-year students were hearing about transfers, new students and their parents had a myriad of questions, and a transition to new leadership had to be smooth. Under the guidance of the Trustees, we worked to complete a successful Endowment Expansion campaign. All of this meant relentless travel as we sought to guarantee the future of Deep Springs College, the small academic oasis in the high desert of Eastern CA.

USU also sought my advice and counsel on how to start and complete the comprehensive fundraising campaign. Closing a $15M endowment campaign for a school with twenty-six students while starting a campaign with a goal of $200M for 20,000 students, was challenging. The art of philanthropy is about relationships and both institutions provided friends enough for many lifetimes.

Annual Deep Springs gatherings in New York and Washington, D.C. gave us an opportunity to see some of the important areas where the Christmas trip might land. We ventured down to Ground Zero in New York to see how the 9/11 cleanup had created space for a new monument.

We noted subways, times, and distances from Central Park. The highlight was presenting one of Deep Springs' most distinguished alumni, Ambassador Willian Vanden Heuvel, with the Deep Springs Medal at his beautiful Penthouse in NYC. As we drove from New York to Washington, D.C., an exit ramp took us to Philadelphia's Citibank Park to see if a hotel for our tour group was within walking distance. We met numerous Deep Springs alumni and parents along the way. Every meeting was bittersweet; our years at Deep Springs had been magical, life changing, and created powerful personal relationships.

On the home front, schedules were changing. Bart and his family were transferred to Southern California with his job. Fred accepted a new job which meant he had not accumulated enough vacation time for our ten day travel schedule. Both families planned to meet us enroute. In the meantime, as the end of June neared, we began to pack for our return to Utah. Honestly, I was apprehensive about leaving Deep Springs in the hands of a new President who fundamentally found student self-governance a bad idea. Students felt otherwise.

Pres. Albrecht put me on the payroll early so I could attend "roll-out" events in Western cities. Once we had the schedules of these events, I also organized lunches or dinners with Deep Springs alumni in the same cities.

Consequently, we had a combined farewell and welcome back tour throughout early June.

By late June, everything was secure except for two NYC events. In both cases, it seemed impossible to get fifty-plus tickets purchased that were relatively close to others in our group. One was a midweek matinee performance of the Broadway musical, "The Lion King," and the second involved tickets to Yankee Stadium. The theatre ticket outlets in New York were a bit sketchy about selling that many young children's tickets at a lower price as well as finding adjacent seats. One evening during dinner at Deep Springs, we were describing our problems and one of the Professors, Matt Fox, asked if he could enlist his sister, who worked on Broadway to help. Idahoans stick together, and within a week his sister found fifty-one tickets on two adjacent rows for less than we anticipated.

Old Yankee Stadium was about to be abandoned for a new "state-of-the-art" replacement, so every game in 2007 was nearly a sellout. Yankee player Alex Rodriquez was also closing in on his 500th career homerun, so the pressure was on to find seats at all. Frustrated, one morning I explained my desire and dilemma to a young man who had just started a job at Stub Hub, the national ticket broker. After going through a lengthy description of why we were doing a Christmas trip in the summer, he said, "You don't need to explain. My job is to get tickets—Christmas, Hanneke, April Fool's Day—it is about the tickets."

"Great perspective," I replied, "but I am close to desperate with the Yankees."

"This is an awesome challenge and I love to do the impossible," he told me one morning while I sat at the table outside the service station in Big Pine.

"Man, if you can do this, I will be forever grateful."

We only had two nights scheduled in New York, so I gave him the credit card number and began the long wait.

The last week of June, my brother, Karl, hooked my cousin, Mont's, large new horse trailer behind Karl's pickup and came to the desert to help us return home with our many belongings. Kay's dearly beloved piano had been a necessity to take to Deep Springs. Dick Dawson, our incredible music teacher from the Owens Valley, came from his home near Bishop every Tuesday at 7:00 a.m. He gave Kay a lesson in our home (the first ones in 43 years!). Now loading the piano in the front of the trailer with ample pads followed by a three-year accumulation of boxes and of books and files, was a bit problematic! That was followed (while I was not watching) by more than a few very large stones that Kay loved and that the students had pirated from Westgard pass as a gift to Kay when she left Deep Springs. Thank heavens the trailer was very large—we got everything in!

When we drove across the cattle guard and out the lane on our final exit from the college, we heard the traditional ringing of the bell which, for ninety years, accompanied all final departures from the beautiful valley. We looked at each other as tears poured from our eyes. As we began the ten-hour trek across some of the loneliest roads in America, we focused totally on the planned Christmas trip. At a gas stop in Tonopah, Nevada, my cell phone rang. Jeff, at Stub Hub, called to report, "Miracle of Miracles—we got 52 tickets in the upper deck down the right field line!" Peace filled my soul.

I started work at USU on July 1, 2007, and ten days later, I went to a doctor's office to have a large lump removed from my lower left bicep. The doctor had examined it a few months earlier and we agreed to wait until our return to Logan before removing it. The doctor assumed it was similar to the one removed from my right forearm thirty years earlier. Then, a bone chip had made its way to the surface encased in fatty tissue.

However, two days after the surgery, he called and bluntly stated, "The biopsy indicated the lump is a malignant tumor and we need more tests to determine the origin and probably recommend either surgery, chemo, or radiation."

I thought for a minute and asked, "Why didn't you take a biopsy while it was still in my arm?"

Doctors often do not like being questioned but he said, "The tumor did not look malignant or at all cancerous." When I got home and told Kay, we agreed that nothing would stand in the way of our Christmas trip. I was not sick and knew that tests and treatment usually meant sickness, so I told the doctor I would come back the second week of August.

Kay and I agreed to not tell any of the travelers. The trip had to go forward. Christmas remained the focal point of our plan. By going in the summer, Kay felt we could emphasize the message instead of the pageants, decorations, presents, and often exhaustion. No "Black Friday" or "Blue Light Specials," just the gift of a trip together. The bus became a visual laboratory of kindness, concern, service, and laughter.

It is impossible to capture the intense period from July 26 to August 5 of 2007. The philosophy was "scratch the surface," create interest, and keep moving. We started in Baltimore (two nights), on to Philadelphia (one night), west to Gettysburg through Amish Country and then southeast to Washington D.C. (two nights). From D.C. it would be a night-time drive to New York (three nights), on to Cooperstown and Springfield (one night) and then to Boston (two nights).

Our main concern was to keep twenty-five children (ages four to eighteen) engaged in what they were seeing and experiencing. Fort McHenry, the Naval Academy, and Camden Yard got us started and Independence Hall, the Liberty Bell, Betsy Ross's house, Citizen's Bank Park, and Valley Forge kept us on course. Gettysburg and the Amish farms and the Memorials on the Mall at night filled up a day. Every child was in awe at the Tomb-of-the-Unknown soldier and Changing-of-the-Guard in Arlington National Cemetery and our special private tour through the Nation's Capitol Building.

Since children under ten were not admitted to the Holocaust Museum, Kay and others who had previously visited the Museum took the seven younger children for a head start at the Smithsonian Museums. After leaving Mount Vernon in the evening, we drove nonstop to New York City while watching the film, "National Treasure," in the bus. Although there was some grumbling over early morning departures, free hotel breakfasts of powdered eggs and frozen waffles, and being at a venue before it opened at 8:00 a.m., all survived.

New York was an absolute delight! The Hotel was an insane place located in a small, but very high building. There were four bedrooms on each floor that surrounded the elevator. The rooms had no space on the floor or between the beds for luggage. The two beds were separated literally by about two feet. I kept everyone tired, and they became used to close quarters.

Our first day in the city was memorable to say the least. At the Empire State Building we were on the first elevator of the day. After that breathtaking tour, we visited Rockefeller Center and St. Patrick's Cathedral before attending the Minskoff Theatre matinee of "The Lion King" on Broadway. Our granddaughter, Aliya, was barely old enough to go to the theatre because the cut-off age was 4 ½ years! However, the children were so in awe of the portrayal of all the animals that they never moved a muscle.

We then jumped onto the subway and went to the Bronx at the old, and soon to be abandoned, original Yankee Stadium (the house that Babe Ruth built!) to watch the Yankees v. Chicago White Sox Baseball game. Although high on the second deck, the fans abused any of our group that wore non-Yankee apparel.

The second day in NYC began with the earliest tour of the Statue of Liberty and Ellis Island, then Battery Park, the tragic site of 9-11, Lincoln Center and Central Park. No one got lost, nor did anyone stand still.

The third morning, Big Bob picked us up at 7:00 to motor north along the Hudson River toward Cooperstown. Bob and I discussed a "short cut" through the Catskills on NY Route 28. It would save us forty-five miles and looked like a beautiful alternative to I-87. The winding route, with much braking, went close to the location of the famous 1969 Woodstock Festival. Maybe those vibes caused most of the bus passengers to experience a major outbreak of motion sickness. Apparently, I had been stern about the departure time and wanted to be first in line at the Baseball Hall of Fame, so no one complained or even dared ask Bob to slow down. When we got there, Gavin, age 5, said, "Bob, you got us here safely." The big fellow teared up.

When one was so close to fulfilling a lifelong dream, the mantra became, "Put the pedal to the metal and let her roll." By 10 a.m. we were in the building, and I soon found myself moving back and forth from Hank Aaron to Warren Spahn and Eddie Mathews. The group spent the entire day at the facility or in the nearby village shops and indulged my personal desire to visit our Mecca. When they kicked us out at closing time, we grabbed some food and turned east toward Springfield, Massachusetts, and prepared for the Basketball Hall of Fame and then eventually on to Boston and Fenway Park.

We have not forgotten the details of the trip, but some deserve close elaboration. At Gettysburg, we contracted with a guide who had spent a career as a Junior High teacher. He dramatically illustrated what happened on this hallowed ground during those hot and humid July days of 1863.

Our guide stopped the bus at the North Carolina monument on Seminary Hill. Gutzen Borglum's statue of North Carolina soldiers is magnificent, and that is where the guide chose five of the youngsters to teach them why it was necessary to have five men at each cannon. Then he asked all the children to count off from 1-4, put them in lines and when he gave the command, all the threes were shot, then the ones, and finally the fours. Only the twos were left standing. He then told them the story of Pickett's charge and that only 25% of the soldiers survived. He had the survivors drag the wounded or dead, back to the cannons. Our guide then stated there would be many empty plates at Christmas dinner.

All of us were reminded that when General Robert E. Lee retreated from Gettysburg and returned to Virginia, he left the wounded in the hands of the Union Army and its surgeons. The families of Gettysburg, despite their own horrendous losses, took care of the casualties with medical attention, sustenance, or burial. The guide noted, "It was as if Christmas came in July." That evening we walked into the Gettysburg cemetery and recited Lincoln's Gettysburg address near the actual spot where he delivered it 144 years before. The children stood in reverence. Sadly, Abraham Lincoln, like 600,000 other American citizens, gave "the last full measure."

Gettysburg was ancient history compared to 9-11. When we went to lower Manhattan to see where a new Memorial would be constructed, there was a giant hole in the ground. The two towers had collapsed, and the hole was symbolic of all those who had died. It was eerie to stand on the ground where only six years earlier those giant towers had been destroyed, with nearly three thousand deaths. At that time, the country was unified in its grief and desire to love one another.

Cooperstown and the Baseball Hall of Fame provided a treasured Christmas moment. For me, because of the pace of our journey, the lingering concern over a tumor had vanished. This small, pristine village in rural New York is to me, a "sacred place," a bit of Heaven-on-Earth. Since 1939, people have gathered to witness the enshrinement of legends, heroes, and even a few scoundrels who could hit or throw a baseball. It is a museum, a memorial, and a place where fans assemble to remember.

Baseball tells the story of much of American history. People go there to debate the selection process, compare the players, and to discuss and disagree. Positive changes in American Society are highlighted by including the stories of the sons of immigrants, sharecroppers, miners, and racial integration. The small facility amidst that village is a slice of history that rivals the intensity of religious fervor. Our family and friends brought Christmas to Cooperstown in the summer of 2007, and we will never forget the day spent there.

It was bittersweet when we all split up for our flights home at Boston Logan Airport. A good tour is evaluated by how sad people are to leave each other after being in close quarters for ten days. The tears and the hugs were many and heartfelt. While waiting for our flight, we saw one of our dear friends from Utah, Doug Foxley, who, after hearing a few particulars, of the tour, shook his head and said, "A trip for the ages—What a gift."

Yes Sir!

Postscript:

Kay took me to the doctor in mid-August and after two months of Cat Scans, MRI's, x-rays, pet scans, nuclear testing, colonoscopy, and endoscopy, the doctors still could not determine the source of the tumor. Stan Albrecht and my staff supported me constantly. My friend, John Miller, interceded and flew us to the Mayo Clinic in Rochester, MN. Dr. Ralph Richardson, went through every test, and after two days, shook his head over certain attempts at diagnosis, ordered a new biopsy, brought in a fellow doctor, and said simply, "They misdiagnosed the type of tumor. You have a Merkel cell carcinoma which remained encased and was removed by the surgery."

Another Christmas gift.

Big Bob with Gavin.

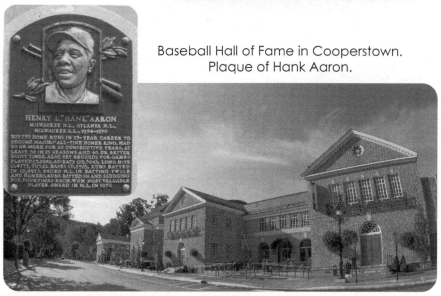

Baseball Hall of Fame in Cooperstown.
Plaque of Hank Aaron.

Learning to shoot a cannon.

On the steps of
the State House in
Boston.

Preparing for Pickett's Charge - Gettysburg.

Old Town Albuquerque

Indian Pueblo Cultural Center

CIVIL RIGHTS AND CHRISTMAS
Written 2016

Perhaps it is time to turn off the mouth and leave professing to a new generation. As I concluded my final lecture in a course on the American Civil Rights Revolution, I choked up. It is not really a good thing for a teacher to exhibit that much passion and emotion. Professors are schooled in objectivity, balance and detachment. But down deep, I realized that this might be my last class and certainly on the topic that has identified me as a teacher. So I let it go as to why this might be the most important class of their lives.

After the class, one of our friends who was auditing the class told us of discussing the class with an acquaintance who asked, "What slant does the Professor take?" There is no slant when you teach the constitutional gospel of inclusion, equality, and participation. There is no slant when you describe the movement in terms of civility, decency, and humility. My lecture closely resembled a sermon, delivered with passionate conviction.

Following class, I walked to the car, tossed my pack in the back, and headed for Mundo's restaurant with three grandchildren who believe they have earned some type of luncheon "scholarship." (They have!) But once again, I choked up and let the tears flow freely.

The Christmas season is upon us and the world seems to be engaged in a chaotic free-fall, defying description. Mass shootings, terrorist attacks, and insane political rhetoric have created an atmosphere of fear and loathing. I cannot think of a time when the message of Civil Rights, accompanied by a Christmas reminder has been more needed.

It is time for me to slow down and think of Christmas. Jesus' life and birth remind us of the divinity and diversity of humanity. Christ is a huge part of the Civil Rights Movement because many of the Civil Rights leaders based their actions and words on the New Testament.

Recently, while on a business trip to Albuquerque, New Mexico, I went into Old Town to see and experience the Christmas season. In two or three small galleries that I visited, there were numerous nativities, many with Native American or Hispanic settings. Years ago I bought Kay a southwestern nativity from New Mexico, and on this day, I saw one that nearly duplicated it.

Each depiction of Jesus' birth, from tiny miniatures, to elaborate and expensive porcelain re-creations, reminded me of the simple story of homeless newlyweds. The young couple were in a strange land, trying to find a place where their baby could safely enter the world. Each artist's depiction gave the nativities great meaning.

When I left Old Town, the Christmas season had engulfed me and I began to visit with the taxi driver, an immigrant from Mali. He called himself Rick, and as usual, I probed for a story. Rick's family had moved from Mali to France, and then later he pursued educational opportunities in Northern California. While in college, he met and later married, a Native American from Taos, New Mexico. After the birth of two children, he yielded to her desire to return to New Mexico. They settled in Albuquerque, enjoyed her family nearby, and though he was still looking for work as an engineer, life was good.

Rick's cell phone interrupted our conversation and he spoke rapidly in French with great concern. When the call ended, he asked me if I minded if we did not go directly to my hotel. A friend from his church was stranded and needed a ride to work or he might lose his job. Rick assured me the stop was on our way. I had a free evening, and so we shared an errand of mercy that I probably paid for twice-over. However, I felt good that he was able to help his friend, another first-generation African American. In Jesus' short lifetime, He stopped many things he was doing to help those in need. Although the nativities focus on Jesus, the baby, His life reflects an eternal appreciation for the Innkeeper who offered the stable and the manger.

The night clerk at my hotel responded to my tap on the courtesy bell. Francisco, the clerk, worked until 2:00 a.m. and then attended the University of New Mexico where he majored in business. In an earlier conversation, he told me he had considered going into Hotel Management because the Hilton chain provided career opportunities for trusted employees. However, he feared the hours and turnover among service workers. He laughed, saying his Spanish could help keep great relations with the workers. I asked to be scheduled for a ride to the airport in the morning, but suddenly the television distracted him. I tried to engage him by asking, "How was your day?" He responded with a question:

"Do you know how long my family has been in New Mexico?"

"No sir, I don't."

"They came from Spain in the 1640's and these clowns," he pointed at the TV, "group any Latino in an alien class and want to deport us all."

"What are you talking about?" I said.

"I have been watching this Presidential debate and I am sorry ... this is not my country."

We visited for half an hour and I told him that I teach Civil Rights and that the success of this nation historically was its commitment to equal opportunity. He just shook his head and said that for the first time in his life, he felt like a stranger. One of his co-workers, an Asian girl from Phoenix, had joined us. She, too, shook her head and commented, "Politics are crazy! They say anything to get votes." And then she asked Francisco, "Do you have time to look over my English essay?"

Francisco looked at me and said, "Amy, we have a professor here, let him help!" Before I could respond, he laughed, said something about his "perfect Spanglish" and they disappeared into an office. My efforts to offer perception and comfort fell on deaf ears as I climbed the stairs to my fourth-floor room.

As I unlocked the door, my thoughts returned to the variety of nativities I had admired that day. The artists had chosen different ethnic groups which, through impressive carving and painting, created a universal representation of the Savior's birth. Then I reflected on the teachings of Jesus. Here was a man raised in a country occupied by a foreign power, with an autocratic King who answered to the Romans and a system of judges who maintained a certain level of internal religious authority. Amid this turmoil, there were many other ethnic groups in some degree of subjugation.

Jesus grew to manhood in that atmosphere and prepared to challenge the power structure in the land of his birth. The babe born in Bethlehem became a man determined to change the world forever and to provide an eternal perspective (which escaped his fellow countrymen). He was described as a rebel, as were many of the Civil Rights leaders. Jesus Christ, Mahatma Ghandi, Martin Luther King, Jr. and Malcolm X all asked people to change, and in the process, to challenge the existing system. From his birth, Jesus created an uncertainty among the establishment. That is why the King tried to slay all of the youngsters—one just might have been the ultimate rebel, the Messiah.

In preparation for the Civil Rights class, I had listened to Martin Luther King's rendition of the story of the Good Samaritan. As I thought of the diverse residents of Albuquerque, the fact that Jesus made the hero of the story a Samaritan gave me pause. In His sermon, King brilliantly explained the status of a despised minority-the Samaritan. They were hated by the Jews and the Romans. Why did the Levite and the Priest pass by the bruised and battered man? Why did the Samaritan stop to give him assistance, place him on a donkey, and prepay for his stay at an inn? Every character had a logical reason to do what they did, or did not do, but the Samaritan saw another human's suffering, and acted. For a "chosen" people who viewed other ethnic groups as inferior, a "Good Samaritan" was not a message they wanted to hear.

Jesus followed the same pattern as He healed the ten lepers and then only one returned to thank the man who erased his affliction. The one leper who returned to give thanks was a Samaritan. A parable, followed by a real-life experience, drove the point home. All of God's children count in His eyes and deserve to be treated as His offspring. When Jesus came across a group of citizens prepared to stone a woman taken in adultery, and the leaders of the group tried to engage Jesus in a debate on the penalty dictated by law, He simply stated, "He that is without sin, cast the first stone." As the accusers departed, Jesus then taught one of the great lessons of his ministry. He asked the woman to "go thy way and sin no more." The beauty of His message is that it changed the way people thought about other people-we are all God's children.

Once I entered room 424, I automatically reached for the remote control, but baseball season was over and I did not want to hear another rehash of the political debate, so the TV remained silent. I recalled some of the people and events of my past in which the message of Christmas rang loud and clear-through actions, not just platitudes or nice music.

My mother told a story of one of the men from our neighborhood who never quite pulled his life together after World War II. He had come home as an alcoholic and could never emerge from the curse of the disease. When he lost control, he was abusive, and his wife and daughter lived in fear. One Christmas, he locked his family inside the house and tried to burn it down. To help him recover, the court ordered him sent to a rehabilitation facility several miles away from his home. When the community and the LDS church tried to figure out his situation and how to work toward a solution, Bishop Phil Hulme always said, "The demons are real, but I only see him as sober and loving and trying." He repeated that remembrance at his funeral.

During the 1950's, polio was a feared and dreaded disease which left its mark on our valley and our family. The victims, including my oldest brother, Karl, were dispatched to St. Anthony's hospital in Pocatello, Idaho where the Catholic sisters served as nurses. At that time, although many believed that polio was communicable, those sisters, fearless and faithful, offered tender care and hope. They were assisted by the African American custodial staff who helped keep the wards sterile and created a joyful atmosphere.

While my mother stayed with Karl in Pocatello, she marveled at the loving attention given the patients. Her prayers were their prayers and the sisters and workers even came to understand and appreciate the blessings given by Mormon elders. From this new experience, Mother taught inclusiveness in the same manner as the Savior. After they had returned home and Christmas neared, her thoughts and gifts went to St. Anthony's as an expression of gratitude.

Finally, my thoughts turned to my father, and I cherished the memory of the absolute pleasure of being able to work side-by-side with him on the farm, in corrals, fencing, and in the ready-mix concrete business. In many respects, his life had not been easy, and he often remained a bit guarded with his inner-most thoughts. His parents divorced when he was young; he almost never lived with either after they split. Fiercely independent and amazingly tough, Dad passionately fought for the underdog.

One year, hunters on our farm decided to shoot at some of the equipment, including a tractor. We did not have much, and on a subsistence farm, equipment was essential. When the young men were apprehended and then confessed, Dad became their advocate in the court. The boys were fatherless, adrift, and facing potential banishment to the State Industrial school in St. Anthony. He literally championed their cause, found them jobs at Christmas and guided them through education, keeping them out of the reform school, and relieving their mother's grieving heart.

That is only one small example, of many, that crossed my mind as I thought of those I know who simply act to help another person in need.

Impulsively, I reached for my cellphone and quickly checked the "Steps" app. I had not had a good walking day or climbed many flights of stairs, and I needed to walk. I put on my shoes, grabbed my jacket and returned to the lobby.

Determined to walk around the parking lot until I reached 10,000 steps, I stopped to hear Francisco talk to an elderly woman. She had the appearance of being homeless and wanted to stay in the lobby to be warm. Tearfully, she claimed she had friends in Albuquerque. Francisco asked her for a phone number and address of a friend in order to confirm the accuracy of her story. There is a distrust of the homeless who ask for money or favors; but he called the number, nodded, and then hung up the phone. To the woman, he said, "Your daughter has been waiting for you. She doesn't have a car, so I am going to call a cab." Francisco called the dispatcher and said, "Is Rick still on duty? Please send him over."

I left the lobby and quickly started lapping the building on my walk. About half way through the second lap, embarrassment overwhelmed me. I returned to the lobby and told Francisco and Amy that I wanted to pay the woman's fare. "No need," he said, "we save the tip money from the complimentary breakfast and any cash that is left in the rooms."

"Please," I answered, "let me help."

Amy answered, "Just ask Rick how much it is and you can help."

Rick pulled up in the green Taurus, jumped out cheerfully and opened the door. I had a feeling that the hotel and the cab driver had done this before. The woman just stared at all of the commotion, saying nothing. Tears ran down her face.

"How much is the fare?" I asked.

Rick chuckled and said, "The meter is off. I am on my way home and this address is on my way."

Laughing, Francisco shook his head. "Rick, you live ten miles north of town, man why not just take the money?" I handed him $20 and he drove away with Christmas music blaring.

It is good to recall what the Savior taught and what He did. His life has inspiration and influence through those who practice His fundamental teachings. My new friends in New Mexico try to sacrifice and save in order to create better opportunities for children, siblings and friends.

There is no end to the need for honest effort and action. Martin Luther King often said that the essence of the Civil Rights movement is found in the 25th chapter of the gospel of St. Matthew. "Inasmuch as ye have done it unto one of the least of these, my BRETHREN, ye have done it unto me."

Jesus Christ lived and taught in a world of restrictive, unjust laws. The Civil Rights Revolution tells us how those statutes cannot keep us from doing what we should do to help our brothers and sisters. It is a simple and just obligation to love one another.

ACKNOWLEDGMENTS

When I decided to publish a second volume of Christmas stories, I knew that the publication of a book is a team effort. As an Historian, I must weigh memory against documented facts. Compared to the earlier book, *Christmas in Montpelier*, which included twelve stories about my childhood in my hometown, this set is more diverse. The stories cover sixty years of adulthood and demonstrate a more serious and reflective tone. This set of stories circulated only among my children and a few friends. I appreciated their suggestions and corrections within the text.

However, a major problem is that through decades, Kay and I accumulated thousands of photographs in a variety of forms. Though there were times when we did not even own a camera, or when we did, both film and developing were too expensive, so much of our lives is undocumented by photographs.

On the other hand, after we obtained cameras and were conscious of events, the number of photographs is numbing. In addition, albums, shoe boxes, plastic tubs, files and envelopes full of photos do get lost or misplaced.

When "iPhones" replaced cameras and unless unintentionally deleted, thousands of images went somewhere in a cloud. Unfortunately, phones are often lost, thus the pictorial aspect of segments of history disappears. My loss of a phone explains why one story has no people in the photos.

Christmas remains a very important part of our lives. It is still a time of family gatherings, giving and receiving, and doing good deeds toward others.

Many of our family members have assisted in preparing this volume. Kylee Peterson, Erin Smoot, and Kate Peterson, granddaughters, helped scan and organize photos, provide technical assistance, and a degree of jocularity.

Our grandson, Anthony, gave a close reading and checked facts. Kay edited the stories when we first presented them, one a year, to the family.

Lisa Godfrey and Patti Mortensen, took the time to read and edit, suggesting kindly that I write in shorter straightforward sentences. My guess is that Kay sought reinforcements to convince me to follow her instructions. (Unfortunately, I did not really follow their subtle suggestions.)

Mickey Fryer, who also designed the first book, is a talented designer who visualizes exactly what the book will be. I value her kind and encouraging suggestions.

In addition, I will always remain thankful that Yvonne and Lee Roderick provide a conduit to the dynamically changing publishing world.

Forever, I pay homage to my esteemed High School English teacher, Lewis Munk, whose writing demands remain embedded in my brain. Learning is an eternal search and others have taught me as well.

In 1976, I wrote a book, *Idaho, A Bicentennial History*. The American Association of State and Local History combined with the National Endowment for the Humanities to publish a book on each state and the District of Columbia in honor of our nation's two hundredth anniversary. Jerry George, the editor, reminded me of how to present a story. Brief, concise, and descriptive were his watchwords and I try to comply. Editors are more than a necessary evil, they save the author from embarrassment by assuming a degree of responsibility for a final draft.

During my fifty-plus years at Utah State University, I have enjoyed many wonderful friends throughout the institution. A decade of service as President, professor, and Trustee at Deep Springs College in California also expanded our circle of friends. A university community is an extended family that is constantly re-energized by new employees and students. Mick and Linda Nicholls came to USU a year before we did. A half century spent together has been a distinct pleasure. Jack and Linda Newell introduced us to Deep Springs and forged a new concept of service which changed our lives.

My current colleagues, Joe Ward, Tammy Proctor, and Patrick Mason, bright stars in the future of Utah State, encourage me to remain upright and continue to serve. Finally, the students we have met and taught deserve thanks as well.

I love what Christmas has meant to me through the years. Kay shares this passion. This holiday provides a focus based on recognizing opportunities to help someone else. What Jesus taught is so simple and direct, but so difficult for humans to do. Christmas reminds us to do and all of those we acknowledge have helped us.

We are so thankful that many of our friends contributed to these stories. They help us create an environment that thrives on relationships and service. Wherever the Petersons go, we embrace the location of our sojourn. Each locale enabled us to learn from new friends and incorporate them into our lives.

Our circle of friends is a gigantic part of these stories. Montpelier, Idaho is still our hometown, and we love it dearly. This love of place, people, the past and the present, enables us to appreciate every place where our heads have rested. We appreciate the beauty and warmth of the locale as well as the people remembered in each of these stories.

ABOUT THE AUTHOR

F. Ross Peterson is a native of Montpelier, Idaho, a small Mormon settlement in the far southeastern corner of the state. One of six children, Ross learned how to work with his family and neighbors to survive at the 6000' elevation of Bear Lake Valley. His parents, Raymond, and Zora, sacrificed considerably to provide educational opportunities for their children. He attended Utah State University, went on a LDS mission to the Great Lakes Region, married Mary Kay Grimes, a Montpelier native, and graduated from USU in 1965. After receiving a PhD in American studies from Washington State University, the small family moved to the University of Texas at Arlington in 1968. They returned to Utah state in 1971.

Inspired by high school and university teachers, Peterson became an historian to teach the love of his mind, American history. He chose more Contemporary America as a specialty and circumstances led him into the fields of African American and Western American history. His favorite class through the years is the History of the Civil Rights movement. There is nothing better than to teach American history through the eyes of those seeking to enjoy equality and inclusion within the grand American experience. Throughout his career he has influenced many students and along with his children and grandchildren, those students provide increased joy.

Peterson served in many capacities at Utah State University including department Head of History, director and founder of the Mountain West Center, Milton R. Merrill Chair in Political science, and Vice President for Advancement. He also became the President of Deep Springs College in California. Kay's role in this assignment in a high isolated desert valley was paramount for success. Deep Springs is a unique educational experiment in eastern California that is designed to prepare students for a life of service. It is also a working cattle ranch which allowed Ross to reconnect with his Idaho roots. This treasured period opened a new world of learning possibilities for a small group of students.

Citizenship requires voluntary service and the Petersons complied in a variety of areas. Twice Ross served as a Bishop in the LDS church. Ross and Kay edited *Dialogue: A Journal of Mormon Thought* for five years. He spent six years on the Utah Humanities Council and chaired it for two years, five years on the Utah State Board of History, and five years on the Spike 150 Commemoration Committee. He has received many awards including a Fulbright Fellowship to Victoria University in New Zealand, The Wayne Aspinall Chair at Colorado Mesa University, Emeriti of the Year at USU, and together, the Petersons were named Citizens of the Year in Cache Valley in 2024.

Ross and Kay are the parents of three sons, Bret, Bart, and Matthew (Fred). They have eleven grandchildren and nine great grandchildren. They still reside in the home in River Heights they purchased in 1971. It is convenient to most of their gathering places, and everyone knows where they are. We have had a blessed life.

Also by F. Ross Peterson

- *A History of Bear Lake Pioneers,* editor
- *Prophet Without Honor: Glen H. Taylor and the Fight For American Liberalism*
- *Idaho: A Bicentennial History*
- "Politics and Protest" in *The Oxford History of the American West* with Michael P. Malone
- *A History of Cache County*
- *Ogden City: Its Governmental Legacy* with Robert Parson
- "Confronting the Desert" in *The Snake: The Plain and Its People*
- *A History of the Central Utah Project* with Robert Parson and Craig Fuller
- "Harry Truman and His Critics: The 1948 Progressives and the Origins of the Cold War." In *Radicalism in Contemporary America.*
- Christmas In Montpelier.

Family at Huntsman Hall, USU - 2017

Julian Petri and Gareth Fisher, Deep Springs, 2004

Coach Kay and Bart, Kenosha, WI 1991

Julie & Bret with colleague Mick & Linda Nicholls, 2004

Ross's Family - Max, Ross, Brent, Donna Lee, Karl, Reed - 2005

Bret, Ross, Fred and Bart - 2007

Jen & Bart, Fred & Kami, Julie & Bret - 1995

Bret, Ross, Bart, Kay, Fred - Old Main Hill - 1996

Family in the back yard at home in River Heights, Utah - 2008

Deep Springs Sunset. - 2005
photo by Kay

Jefferson Memorial - 2007

Washington Monument - 2007

"Mookie" - 1995
(Ross & Kay's youngest child)

Kay Peterson - 1989
"I wonder what he (Ross) is up to now?"

Grandchildren - 2009

Grand Marshals at USU Homecoming Parade - 2015

Emeriti of the Year, 2021, Utah State University.

Commencement Speaker at Deep Springs, 2001.

The cost of admission to the Summer Citizen's Picnic -
one can of Dr. Pepper - 1992

Kay with
Jo (sister),
and Gean
(mother).

Annie Miller,
Ross & Kay,
2000.

John Hill and Ross - 1994
Bennion Workshop - USU

Rob & Shauna Robinson - 1994
Bennion Workshop - USU

Ross conferring Master's Degree to April Jensen - Dec 2009.

Justin Kim, Andrew Kim, Kay - Deep Springs, Jan 2001.
Andrew - Senator from New Jersey - 2024

Abiola - photo by Kay - 2005

Larry (Kay's brother), Ross, Kay, Peggy (Larry's wife) -
Cooperstown - 2007

Made in the USA
Columbia, SC
04 December 2024

47326235R00124